Morality a... Revisited

Morality and Architecture Revisited

DAVID WATKIN

JOHN MURRAY
Albemarle Street, London

Frontispiece: Swiss Re Headquarters, London – Photomontage view of Tower from St Helen's Courtyard West. Architects Foster and Partners. Photograph by Richard Davies.

First published in 2001
by John Murray (Publishers) Ltd,
50 Albemarle Street, London W1S 4BD

A catalogue record for this book is available from the British Library

ISBN 0-7195-6404 2

Typeset in 11/13 Monotype Bembo by Servis Filmsetting Ltd
Printed and bound in Great Britain by Butler & Tanner Ltd,
London and Frome

Contents

Preface[1]

The world out of which *Morality and Architecture* grew was the 1960s and 70s, years which are now widely seen as a time when untold damage was done to British towns and cities through the destruction of historic street patterns by the aggressive imposition of concrete tower-blocks and inner-city ring roads. All this was dependent on Corbusier's 'Plan Voisin' of 1925 which proposed the destruction of an historic area of central Paris from Montmartre to the river Seine, replacing it with a grid of eighteen high-rise tower-blocks. This was to form a fit setting for the modern man who had finally destroyed the past, an image dear to architects of the International Modern Movement.

After the Second World War, this alarming model was put into practice in towns and cities throughout the world in new buildings which, taking the place of the old terraced houses in Britain, were designed with total lack of attention to their environment, to traditional forms, materials, or patterns of living. One of the most disastrous examples was Chandigarh, capital of the Punjab, India, built by Le Corbusier in the 1950s and 60s in response to Nehru's call for a city which would be 'unfettered by the traditions of the past'.[2] As the Prince of Wales daringly said in a speech to the Corporation of the City of London at the Mansion House in 1987, post-war planners and developers had done more damage to our cities than war-time bombing by the Luftwaffe. A typical example

---

[1] I am indebted for their comments on the first draft of new material in this book to Dr Richard John and Professor Roger Scruton.
[2] Norma Evenson, *Chandigarh*, Berkeley and Los Angeles, 1966, p. 6.

would be the work of James Stirling of 1967–76 at Runcorn New Town where rows of flats with circular windows resembling launderettes created a social brutality matching their architectural brutality, so that, in common with many other housing developments of their period, they have had to be demolished. Welcoming Runcorn New Town in his influential *Buildings of England* series, Sir Nikolaus Pevsner went so far as to devote an entire page to its plan, at a time when the volumes had no plans.[3] Though planning of this kind was often commercially driven, there was a philosophy behind it which required destruction of the past to make a scientific rational setting for modern man. It was associated with a belief in the need to be 'frankly modern' by rejecting tradition so as to build 'in the style of the time'; to opt out would be to 'falsify history'.

I found that the philosophy behind this was associated with a Hegelian *Zeitgeist* which lay behind the promotion of modernism by Pevsner. *Morality and Architecture* was thus an attempt to explain why it is unnecessary to accept the vacuous philosophy which lies behind modernism. Taking on the establishment, the book caused a considerable stir at the time, receiving passionate praise and passionate criticism. Why bring it out again, twenty-four years later? The reason is simply that, though the general public is as hostile now as it was then to the damaging effects of modernist architecture in historic settings, the professional architectural establishment is still dominated by the same beliefs. Then as now, the practice of traditional and classical architecture is taught in no British school of architecture.

Moreover, the blind worship of the new, which seemed to be fading in the 1980s, received a powerful fresh impetus as we approached the year of the millennium. This hatred of the past, associated with constant assault on what was identified in every field of endeavour as 'the forces of conservativism', led to the unexpected promotion in the 1990s of old High Tech architects

---

[3] Nikolaus Pevsner and Edward Hubbard, *The Buildings of England, Cheshire*, Harmondsworth 1971, p. 326.

such as Norman Foster and Richard Rogers who, as a result, now totally dominate the architectural scene in 2001. Rogers, despite some sensible ideas on planning and traffic, believes that his buildings point to a future in which 'architecture will no longer be a question of mass and volume but of lightweight structures whose superimposed transparent layers will create form so that architecture will be dematerialised'. Norman Foster's Millennium Bridge, the 'wobbly bridge', is doubtless an excellent example of 'dematerialised' architecture.

Modern buildings which have been popular with the general public include products of the 'will to shock' aesthetic such as Frank Gehry's spectacular Guggenheim Museum in Bilbao. However, these are examples of a prima-donna aesthetic, one-off monuments of display which do not provide a helpful model for the creation of a humane urban environment. More relevant in that context are the underground stations on the Jubilee Line Extension in London and the similar winged railway stations and airports by Santiago Calatrava in France and Spain which boldly develop the flying glass and iron roofs of Victorian railway stations.

To return to the 1960s and 70s, few architects were able to resist the stranglehold of modernism, for it was then virtually impossible to receive any commissions without conforming to it. Those who did, notably Francis Johnson, Marshall Sisson, Claude Phillimore, Philip Jebb, and Raymond Erith, produced buildings of which, as John Martin Robinson explained, the majority were 'never . . . published in the architectural press and hardly recorded in Nikolaus Pevsner's *Buildings of England* series'.[4] He recounts the story of how, 'in 1983, the leading architectural magazine, the *Architectural Review*, refused to publish Quinlan Terry's pavilion at Thenford in Northamptonshire [commissioned by Michael Heseltine] because it is a Classical building'.

Two turning points, moments on my road to Damascus, were, first, visiting Portman Square in March 1963 and scribbling in my

---

[4] John Martin Robinson, *The Latest Country Houses*, London 1984, p. 7.

copy of Pevsner's *London* a note to the effect that half of the south side of this Georgian square was in the process of demolition and that the whole of the west side, though still intact, was empty and awaiting demolition. It was not that these houses were of outstanding quality but that undoubtedly whatever took their place would be far worse and would reject every value that they stood for. On the site of the houses on the west side now stands the abysmal Churchill Hotel.

A second turning point which determined me to take up the cudgels against the architectural establishment world was the influential welcome given by Pevsner to the new buildings which violated British towns, such as Lord Holford's Paternoster Square (1961–67), next to St Paul's Cathedral. Here, Holford wanted, in his own words, 'no harmony of scale, character, or placing, just a total contrast'. Though this historic area of London had been devastated by fire on several occasions, 961, 1087, the Great Fire of 1666, and the Blitz of 1940, on each time except the last, its dense network of streets and lanes survived to find new vitality and prosperity. Holford destroyed the traditional relationship between the Cathedral and the City by providing tall office buildings with priority given to vehicles at ground level, though with the occasional windy pedestrian deck or 'precinct'. His high-rise blocks, one of them eighteen storeys high, provided only three-quarters of the accommodation that existed in the traditional four- and five-storey buildings on the site before the Second World War. There was no reason or pressure to build high, for the required density could have been achieved with lower buildings laid out on a different plan: the tower blocks were selected entirely from reasons of fashion. Holford's Paternoster Square was praised by Pevsner as an 'outstandingly well conceived precinct'.[5]

Another sensitive area of London, which owed everything to the brilliant town planning of John Nash, is now dominated by New Zealand House (1959–63), a tower-block by Robert Matthew,

---

[5] Nikolaus Pevsner, *London*, I, *The Cities of London and Westminster* (1957), rev. ed., Harmondsworth 1973, p. 285.

Johnson-Marshall & Partners. It wrecks the grain of a whole area including Lower Regent Street, Waterloo Place, and Pall Mall East, which, though harmoniously rebuilt by later architects, preserves the Regency flavour of Nash's attempt to bring classical dignity to the centre of London. Pevsner devoted an astonishingly long enco-mium of seventeen lines to this building which he described as 'an excellent example of the commendable type of office build-ing . . . placed in a well-chosen position'.[6]

At John Belcher's rich and delicately carved Institute of Chartered Accountants (1890) in the City of London, William Whitfield's additions of 1964–70 included a giant aggressive block of which Pevsner similarly wrote: 'the concrete surfaces heavily reeded, a windowless staircase expressed by its very steps showing. Here is proof, if proof were needed, that the uncompromisingly new can go with the old . . .'[7]

To emphasize his rejection of tradition, Pevsner prefaced his section on modern architecture in the City of London with the statement that, 'As for architecture proper, it ought to be recorded first that the neo-classical, neo-Georgian spectre is even now not yet laid'.[8] The examples he condemned included modern classical buildings by McMorran and Whitby which I particularly admired: Wood Street Police Station of 1966 and their extension to the Old Bailey of 1972. The image of laying a spectre struck me then, as now, as offensive: burying a tradition was, after all, the language of Khruschev to Kennedy in his ugly, and false, boast, 'we will bury you'.

To conclude this Preface, *Morality and Architecture* appears again in 2001 because the philosophy it exposed is still current. Even on its publication in 1977, the opponents of the book pretended that modernist doctrines were no longer widely held. Charles Jencks claimed that 'David Watkin charges out on to the field . . . finds an enemy and with perfect aim delivers a mortal blow. But lo, the

---

[6] *Ibid.*, p. 589.
[7] *Ibid.*, p. 246.
[8] *Ibid.*, p. 111.

enemy is already dead.'[9] However, the insensitive placing of individual high-rise blocks in historic areas of London which, so dominant in the 1960s, had receded during the growing conservation
movement from the 1980s, has now returned with a vengeance in
London. Instead of grouping such towers coherently in new settings such as Canary Wharf, it is now proposed to raise them over
mainline and underground railway stations. The City of London
is threatened by Norman Foster's Swiss Re tower, the 'gherkin'
skyscraper overshadowing the ancient church of St Helen,
Bishopsgate, and by the London Bridge Tower by Renzo Piano and
Broadway Malyon, which would be the tallest office building in
Europe. The Victoria and Albert Museum is threatened by
Libeskind's 'Spiral', resembling a cascade of falling cardboard boxes.
Surviving skylines in the City and the West End of London will be
wrecked for, unlike its continental counterparts, London has no
coherent plan for preserving its skyline. Nor is there any functional
need for high-rise blocks, similar density normally being achievable
through configurations of low-rise buildings.

At the time of writing conservation groups are opposing designs
for the aggressively modernist building which St John Wilson proposes to add the finest early Georgian house in Chichester, Pallant
House. All the old 'frankly modern' arguments are still brought out
in defence of his designs, while the notion that one might follow,
in Alberti's manner, an existing local model is dismissed on all sides
as 'pastiche'.[10] This word is used in a pejorative sense as though it
were always wrong and somehow false to build within a tradition
or to revive an old one. Alberti, in *On the Art of Building in Ten
Books*, gives a stern warning which modernist architects, while

---

[9] Lord Esher said that my ideas were 'redundant' because the theory I criticized
had disappeared and had 'nothing much left of it now but period charm' (*RIBA
Journal*, February 1978). However, writing in *Architecture Australia* in January 1979,
pp. 67–9, Michael Jorgensen defended me from Jencks' criticism that it had all been
said before.

[10] The word pastiche, which does not appear in the *Concise Oxford Dictionary*,
simply connotes something 'composed in the style of a famous author or artist',
according to the *Complete Oxford Dictionary*.

paying lip service to him, have consistently avoided: 'Finally, I advise you never to let greed for glory impel you to embark rashly on anything that is unusual or without precedent. Everything that is to be realised must be weighed and considered in the minutest detail.' Alberti proceeds to set this in the context of the architect who is called on to continue an existing building: 'the innovative architects who follow, strive by all means to make some alteration, and take pride in it; as a result, something begun well by another is perverted and finished incorrectly. I feel that the original intentions of the author, the product of mature reflection, must be upheld.'[11]

---

[11] Leone Battista Alberti, *On the Art of Building in Ten Books* (1482 & 1486), J. Rykwert *et al.*, trans. Cambridge, Mass., and London 1988, pp. 318–19.

PROLOGUE

The Philosophic Background

The Spirit of the Age: Truth in Architecture

As a pupil of Sir Nikolaus Pevsner in the Cambridge School of Architecture, dominated and largely created by the leading modern architect Sir Leslie Martin (1908–2000), I was educated in an architectural context coloured by relentless pressure for modernism and total opposition to any continuation of traditional design. This was typified in Leslie Martin's scheme for the destruction of a vast number of buildings of high quality and interest in and near Whitehall.[12] I came increasingly to question the intellectual foundations on which much of this world rested and the moral high ground occupied by its inhabitants who promoted their preferred architectural style on the supposedly ethical grounds that it should be 'truthful' and should be an 'honest' expression of 'the spirit of its age'.

I thus gave a lecture at Cambridge University in 1968 called 'From Pugin to Pevsner' in which I linked the Gothic Revival architect and theorist A.W.N. Pugin (1812–52) with Pevsner. I did so on the grounds that, seeing architecture and design as instruments of moral and social reform, they had respectively promoted Gothic and Modern Movement architecture to the exclusion of all else in contemporary architecture. No one was allowed to opt out of what each proposed as a total package enforced with something closely approaching moral sanctions. This was combined with a determinist belief that particular architectural forms have a relationship only with a specific time and place. As a result of the continuing influence

---

[12] Leslie Martin, *Whitehall: A Plan for a National and Government Centre*, 1965.

of these two doctrines, it is widely considered to be intellectually indefensible to oppose the intrusion of modernist buildings into the heart of English historic towns and cities.

By contrast, the greatest architectural thinker of the Renaissance, Leon Battista Alberti (1404–72), had urged, as we have seen, that when completing a building an architect would be wise to follow the original style. Modernist architectural doctrine condemns such a practice as 'pastiche', insisting that additions to historic buildings should always be 'frankly modern'. The survival of this doctrine is one of the reasons why *Morality and Architecture*, the book which grew out of my lecture of 1968, is now reissued at a time when the need to reinstate an historical sense, by questioning the myth of 'modern man' who had nothing to learn from the past[13] is as necessary as ever.

In 1976 I sent the typescript of this book for his opinion and advice to Professor Gombrich. He encouraged me by writing to me in a long letter that,

> I am with you in principle, and I could not but agree with the basis of your argument. After all, you have been kind enough to call on me as a witness and I stand by what I have said on these and other occasions about the wrongheadedness and sometimes the pompous fatuity of 'historicist' arguments.

I had particularly asked him about the problem I faced of publishing sustained criticism of a living author, Pevsner. He wondered whether I 'might look at people like Pevsner more charitably' if I considered that 'functionalism can be interpreted as a religious architecture, celebrating the religion of progress'. He pointed out that 'at least he has a faith and is no cynic or time-server.' That was true but was scarcely enough to make me relent, particularly when Gombrich went on to point out that,

---

[13] For a fuller account of this, see my essay, 'The Recovery of Reverence', *Architecture and Urbanism for the European City: A Vision of Europe*, G. Tagliaventi and L. O'Connor, eds., Bologna 1992, pp. 25–40.

What is wrong in the ideology of functionalism is the pretence to be 'scientific', to be based on knowledge rather than faith. (It has this in common with Marxism and other recent ideologies.) Granted that it has all the arrogance of religious movements, the faith that it must be right and that it will win because the God of history is on its side, this does not make it bad architecture or even a bad religion.[14]

While awaiting with some apprehension the publication of *Morality and Architecture* I was also hugely reassured by a trenchant essay called 'The Uses and Abuses of Art History', published in March 1977[15] by Francis Haskell who had taught History of Art in Cambridge when I was an undergraduate. Indeed, I succeeded him as Librarian of the Art History Department at Cambridge in 1967 when he left to take up the chair of Art History at Oxford. The principal object of criticism in his essay of March 1977 was *Princes and Artists: Patronage and Ideology of Four Habsburg Courts 1517–1653* (1976) by Hugh Trevor-Roper, whom he roundly condemned for his historical determinism, based on reliance on the *Zeitgeist*: the very reason for which I was daring to criticize Pevsner. For example, Haskell criticized the interpretation by Hugh Trevor-Roper[16] of the Escorial, the great monastery palace commissioned by Philip II of Spain. For Haskell, Trevor-Roper here typified 'The historian [who] seeks to find in the visual arts an exact, almost simplistic, equivalent to the ideas he has formed (rightly or wrongly) about the nature of the patron or the "spirit of the age"'. Haskell thus asked,

why should the 'geometrical severity of the Escorial' have been 'the architectural corollary of the fierce *autos de fe* of Seville and Valladolid?' . . . Is there some general equation between geometrical severity and the treatment of heresy?

---

[14] Professor Sir Ernst Gombrich to the author, 5 April 1976.

[15] In *New York Review of Books*, 17 March 1977, pp. 6–10.

[16] As Lord Dacre of Glanton, Trevor-Roper was Master of Peterhouse, Cambridge, from 1980 to 1987.

Haskell advanced the likelier and simpler explanation that, in common with many other patrons, Philip II was merely 'keen to keep abreast of a purified Italian manner'. He also suggested that Philip's philosophy and his love of the rich work of Titian 'were indeed intimately connected but were antithetical'.[17]

1968, when I delivered the lecture which turned into *Morality and Architecture* was, of course, a year of revolution in the USA and Europe, especially in universities, and I am pleased to have contributed in my own way to the overthrow of orthodoxy. Two years later, on my election to a Research Fellowship at Peterhouse, Cambridge, in 1970, I found myself in a college where academic debate about topics such as the entanglement of religion and politics, was central to the historical research and teaching of Fellows whom I met on a daily basis. They included Sir Herbert Butterfield (1900–79), the historian who had produced the seminal book, *The Whig Interpretation of History* (1931), and *Christianity and History* (1949); Edward Shils (1910–95), an American sociologist and political writer, immensely learned and well read in European literature and political thought; Brian Wormald (b. 1912), author of *Clarendon: Politics, History and Religion* (1951); Maurice Cowling (b. 1926), prolific author of books on political philosophy; Edward Norman (b. 1938), whose Reith Lectures in 1978 were a devastating onslaught on the secular liberal orthodoxies of Anglican bishops; and Roger Scruton (b. 1944), the brilliant polymath and philosopher who was later to publish *The Aesthetics of Architecture* (1979). Against such a background, I gradually converted my lecture of 1968 into the book published in 1977.

In this process I was greatly aided by Professor Shils who made comments, in green ink and nearly illegible, on every page of the original typescript of my book, all of which I incorporated. Cowling, at once more conservative and more anarchic than Shils, later explained how 'Shils's interest in universities, public education, ideologies, intelligentsia and social cohesion, slid easily into an interest in religion which began early as an interest in religious as

---

[17] *Ibid.*, p. 8.

well as political sects.' An admirer of the conservative philosophy of George Santayana (1863–1952), Shils represented, as Cowling put it, 'an informal, undogmatic, morally respectable, secular, liberal conservativism which respected religion as a form of ideology'.[18]

In the brief Prefatory Note to *Morality and Architecture*, I acknowledged my debt to both Shils and to Butterfield's *The Whig Interpretation of History* (1931), the classic exposure of the belief in an unfolding and progressive logic in history. Though Cowling had not read any drafts of my book, I was certainly influenced by his criticism of the secular moralizing of the modern world in two books which he published in 1963, *The Nature and Limits of Political Science* and *Mill and Liberalism*. In these powerful onslaughts on the pseudo-religious solemnities of establishment liberalism, particularly as expressed in the writings of John Stuart Mill, Cowling argued that the liberalism on which the modern world prided itself was in fact a rigid moralizing orthodoxy, frequently narrower in its prescriptions than the religious certainties which it had replaced. Cowling described how

arbitrary certainties appropriate to religion were maintained by an intellectual interest which lacked a church, a special revelation or any particular God. A religion, however, with these conveniences, is a religion nonetheless; its priests, secular by profession, high-minded by inclination and dissenting sometimes by manner and tradition, affected an authority in distributing moral and practical advice even more extensive than the religion they had abandoned.[19]

Pevsner, it now seemed to me, could be identified as one of Cowling's secular priests: he predicted what style ought to be adopted in the twentieth century on the basis of his own moral and sociological imperatives. He interpreted the styles of the past as the

---

[18] [Maurice Cowling], obituary of Edward Shils, *The Times*, 28 January 1995, p. 23.

[19] Maurice Cowling, *The Nature and Limits of Political Science*, Cambridge 1963, pp. 8–9.

inevitable outcome of what he conceived as their social and political *Zeitgeist*. He seemed unaware that his position constituted a classic example of an intellectual outlook described, and condemned, as 'historicism' by Sir Karl Popper and Sir Ernst Gombrich.[20]

Popper and Pevsner were both born in 1902, in Vienna and Leipzig respectively, Gombrich seven years later in Vienna. Of Jewish descent, all three came to England in the 1930s to seek refuge from racial persecution, though Popper and Pevsner were Lutherans. Both Popper and Gombrich thought deeply about the intellectual origins and cultural implications of the Marxist socialism and the National Socialism which had done much to disrupt their lives. The writings of Pevsner, by contrast, do not explicitly refer to these topics: indeed, his art-historical approach remained the classic German one of neo-hegelian *Geistesgechichte*, the obsession with the 'spirit of the age'.

This art-historical approach went back ultimately to Johann Joachim Winckelmann (1717–68), who implied that architectural forms are the expression of the spirit of a country or race, and of the cultural and political circumstances of their day. Modernists go on to argue from this that such forms cannot therefore properly be reused in other places and times; hence their stress on novelty and newness. However, the notion of revival, of looking back to a lost age, can be found even in antiquity. The Hellenistic world under Alexander the Great revived the forms of fifth-century Athens, a process which was followed by the Romans, the Emperor Augustus, for example, echoing the Parthenon frieze in the Ara Pacis of 13–19BC. Vitruvius, author of the only architectural treatise to survive from the classical world, was motivated by a dislike of modern architecture and by a wish to return to a Hellenic and early Republican language.

For Winckelmann, art is an expression of the Idea, a divine force, in which individual Greek artists are of less significance than the reflection of the Greek spirit. This spirit is essentially that of

---

[20] See David Watkin, 'Sir Nikolaus Pevsner: A Study in Historicism', *Apollo*, September 1992, pp. 168–172.

freedom, for he attributed the uniquely sensual beauty of Greek art not only to what he claimed were the environmentally favourable conditions of Greece and Asia Minor, but also to the freedom expressed in the democratic political constitutions of ancient Athens. He stated that, 'The thoughts of the whole people grew higher with freedom, just as a noble branch rises from a sound stock', emphasizing that, 'The freedom which gave birth to great events . . . planted, as it were in the very production of these effects, the germ of noble and elevated sentiments'.[21] Elsewhere he claimed that, in Athens, 'after the expulsion of the tyrants, a democratic form of government was adopted, in which the entire people had a share, the spirit of each citizen became loftier than that of the other Greeks, and the city itself surpassed all other cities . . . [so that] good taste was now generally diffused'.[22]

Believing of art that its 'fate had always been the same as that of Athens,'[23] led him to denigrate art produced under the monarchical or imperial regimes of the Hellenistic world and the Roman Empire. As Potts has shown, 'With Winckelmann, art itself, rather than the figure of a great ruler, became the entity defining a classic period.'[24] He thus believed that great art could not emerge from the world of court culture, arguing that, 'If it had been possible to restore art to its former brilliance it would have been done by Hadrian, who possessed the requisite knowledge, and spared no exertions for the purpose; but the spirit of liberty had departed from the world, and the source which had given birth to lofty thoughts and glorious deeds had disappeared.'[25] Of course the lament over the supposed decline in modern culture was a favourite theme in Roman literature. Winckelmann thus noted with satisfaction that Pliny said that art ended shortly after the death of Alexander the

---

[21] Johann Winckelmann, *History of Ancient Art*, trans. G.H. Lodge, 2 vols, London 1881, vol. i, pp. 292–3.

[22] *Ibid.*, p. 163.

[23] *Ibid.*, vol. ii, p. 212.

[24] Alex Potts, *Flesh and the Ideal: Winckelmann and the Origins of Art History*, New Haven & London, 1994, p. 56.

[25] Winckelmann, *op. cit.*, vol. ii, p. 338.

Great, and that Tacitus asserted that, 'after the battle of Actium, Rome ceased to produce any more great men'; as though to confirm this, Winckelmann added that 'after the death of Augustus the Roman language and eloquence suddenly deteriorated.'[26]

The philosopher Georg Wilhelm Friedrich Hegel (1770–1831) shares with Winckelmann the claim of being the 'father of art history'. Hegel summoned up

> the inner architect of history, the eternal and absolute Idea, which realises itself in humanity . . . [and in] the different national spirits . . . [whose] conflict would be the theatre in which the pageant of history would unfold and move forwards in continuous development.[27]

Believing that the human mind progresses over time, ascending to higher stages of self-understanding, Hegel saw a spiral of progress reflected in artistic creation which is seen as the inevitable expression of the spirit of the age.[28] It is the task of the art historian to disclose this artistic spirit and of the historian to disclose the philosophy of an age. With their stress on the role of the nation or the collective, both thus practise a technique which is inspired by collectivism. The individual work of art must be understood as a symptom of its social and cultural context, including the class or race which produced it. Hegel, for example, sees the Gothic style as the inevitable outcome of feudalism or scholasticism, as well as interpreting all three as simply different expressions of the same spirit.

Regarding the French Revolution as an event of cosmic significance, Hegel was also an admirer of Napoleon, whom he saw as one of 'these business managers of the World Spirit [whose task is] to be aware of the necessary next step to be taken by their world, to make this step their aim and to devote their energy to this.' He

---

[26] *Ibid.*, p. 240.

[27] G.W.F. Hegel, *Aesthetics: Lectures on Fine Art*, trans. T.M. Knox, 2 vols, Oxford 1975, ii, p. 1065.

[28] For an exposure of this kind of philosophical historicism or determinism, see Karl Popper, *The Open Society and its Enemies* (1945), rev. ed., London & New York, 2 vols, 1966.

explained that, 'They represent, as it were, the next species which had already been prefigured internally.'[29] As Gombrich points out, great artists form part of this 'anticipation of the future in the present' in which

> whatever the World Spirit may be aiming at, it must be something new. Thus the old is being devalued while the unknown and untried at least carries within itself the possibility of harbouring the seeds of the future.[30]

From now on, the art historian, a product of the intellectual climate created by Winckelmann and Hegel, could also become a herald of the new epoch, in which capacity he played an enormous part in promoting the Modern Movement in architecture. Karl Popper sought to demonstrate, perhaps too contentiously, what he saw as the dangerous use by thinkers from Plato to Marx of historicist technique to predict the future course of human history.[31]

Pevsner was not, and did not regard himself as, a philosopher in a line inherited from Winckelmann and Hegel, but we now know, as I did not when I wrote *Morality and Architecture*, that he directly inherited this tradition from someone who was in that line, his doctoral supervisor at Leipzig University, Professor Wilhelm Pinder (1878–1947).[32] Pinder first lectured on 'The Englishness of English

---

[29] E. Gombrich, '"The Father of Art History": A Reading of the Lectures on Aesthetics of G.W.F. Hegel (1770–1831)', in *Tributes: Interpreters of our Cultural Tradition*, Oxford 1984, p. 66.

[30] *Ibid.*, p. 67. On these 'world-historical individuals', see also Walter Kaufmann, *Hegel: Reinterpretation, Texts, Commentary*, London 1966.

[31] Karl Popper, *The Open Society and its Enemies*, vol. i, *The Spell of Plato* (1945), 5th rev. ed. London 1966.

[32] See Marlite Halbertsma, *Wilhelm Pinder und die deutsche Kunstgeschichte*, Worms 1992 (first published in Dutch in 1985), and her startling article, 'L'eredità di Wilhelm Pinder: Nikolaus Pevsner e la fine di una tradizione', in Fulvio Irace, ed., *Nikolaus Pevsner: La trama della storia* (Milan 1992, pp. 71–92). In this article she showed how Pinder spoke at the Nazi Rally in Leipzig in 1933 and wrote an encomium for Hitler's birthday in 1939. Pevsner, nonetheless, dedicated to Pinder his *Academies of Art Past and Present* in 1940.

Art' in 1931, a topic on which Pevsner later published a book, suggesting that artists are trapped in the art forms of their native country and in the Zeitgeist. In *Architektur als Moral* (Lepizig 1938), Pinder argued that 'great architecture is always the face of a superindividual whole. In great periods when ideology triumphs, architectural accomplishments are commissioned by the whole community and therefore will be morally good. It should be the countenance of the *Volk*'.

The belief in progress in which everyone sees himself merely as part of a link in a moving chain is a Hegelian doctrine which Pevsner inherited from writers such as Pinder. It was first categorised as Historicism in a paper which Karl Popper delivered at Professor F.A. von Hayek's seminar at the London School of Economics in 1936. Expanded into three articles in 1944–45 in the philosophical periodical, *Economica*, the paper was first published in book form in Italian in 1954 and in English in 1957 as *The Poverty of Historicism*.

For Popper, who had studied the philosophy of society and politics from Heraclitus and Plato to Hegel and Marx, by way of Comte and Mill, ' "Historicism" [is] an approach to the social sciences which assumes that historical prediction is their principal aim, and which assumes that this aim is attainable by discovering the "rhythms" or the "patterns", the "laws" or the "trends" that underlie the evolution of history . . . [historicism is] the view that the story of mankind has a plot and that if we can succeed in unravelling this plot we shall hold the key to the future.'[33] He claimed that 'Every version of historicism expresses the feeling of being swept in to the future by irresistible forces', and that 'Historicism claims that nothing is of greater importance than the emergence of a really new period'.[34]

That Pevsner belongs to this tradition could not be made clearer than by the following statement in the Preface to his book, *Academies of Art Past and Present* (1940):

---

[33] Karl Popper, *Conjectures and Refutations: The Growth of Scientific Knowledge*, 1963, p. 342.
[34] Karl Popper, *The Poverty of Historicism* (1957), London 1972, pp. 160 and 10.

Only by throwing into relief the individual oneness of any given period or style or nation, and the logical coherence of all its utterances in the most varied fields of human activity, will the historiographer in the end be able to make his reader discover what form a certain problem must take at the present moment.[35]

Later in the same book, Pevsner's determinist collectivist view and his associated belief in the *Zeitgeist*, derived from Pinder, were boldly expressed in his claim that:

The illuminated manuscripts of the Reichenau, the sculptures of Reims, Giotto's frescoes were not created because of the existence of a live workshop tradition, but because of a Zeitgeist expressing itself in religion, politics, and philosophy, in guild and in workshop.[36]

Pevsner believed that a dominating and collectivist cultural unity, similar to the one he thought he had found in the Middle Ages, could be discerned in the Modern Movement and especially in the famous early-twentieth-century German school of architecture, the Bauhaus. His principal, perhaps only, work with a conventional scholarly basis, *Academies of Art Past and Present*, though it appears to be an objective historical study, contains a plot which builds up, somewhat incongruously, to the Bauhaus. Under the direction of Walter Gropius and Mies van der Rohe, the Bauhaus represented for Pevsner the climax of the new spirit of collectivism and worship of modernity. Gropius was still writing in 1968 of 'my dream of *total* architecture' which was to 'make it possible for a work group . . . to begin the important process by which a genuine *Zeitgeist* expression, [different] from the I-cult, can develop.'[37] At the Bauhaus, Pevsner argued, one 'might grasp the essence of the new building conception and help to evolve that new style which

---

[35] Nikolaus Pevsner, *Academies of Art Past and Present*, Cambridge 1940, p. 9.

[36] *Ibid.*, p. 224.

[37] Walter Gropius, *Apollo in the Democracy: The Cultural Obligation of the Architect*, New York 1968, pp. 9–10.

can only originate from the will of a whole nation.' In this interpretation he followed Wilhelm Pinder who saw the Bauhaus as an
essentially German expression of design.

Just as Marlite Halbertsma's devastating study of Pinder in 1985
clarified the roots of Pevsner's *Zeitgeist* doctrines, so the no less
shocking book published four years later by Elaine E. Hochman,
Architects of Fortune: Mies van der Rohe and the Third Reich, took a
little further the links which I had drawn between these doctrines
and those of Nazism. Hochman now argued that,

> For Hitler – no less than for his contemporaries, Mies and Gropius –
> architecture was an expression of the central spirit of an
> epoch . . . For them all, architecture both waged the war and assured
> the victory.[38]

She pointed to

> the striking resemblance of the motivating and dynamic forces that
> underlay his [Mies van der Rohe's] style (and by implication of all
> architectural modernity) – its idealism, depreciation of empirical
> reality, absolutism, and arrogance – to the principles that supported
> the Third Reich.

She suggested that they all believed that, behind the inconsistencies
and absurdities of daily life, there 'lay something called "Truth", or
"the Good", or, as Mies was fond of saying, "the spirit of the age".
This alone was what mattered: this alone defined the age . . . For
Mies, it was his architectural ideal; for the Nazis, it was the State.
Within this framework the individual . . . counted for little.'[39]

Pevsner, similarly impressed by what he called the 'overpowering collective energy'[40] of our age, went on to suggest that 'if there

---

[38] Elaine S. Hochman, *Architects of Fortune: Mies van der Rohe and the Third Reich*,
New York 1989, p. 192.

[39] *Ibid.*, pp. 315–16. In *Morality and Architecture*, p. 97, I had drawn attention to the
close parallels between the denigration of the individual by Mies van der Rohe
and by Goebbels.

[40] Nikolaus Pevsner, *Pioneers of the Modern Movement*, London 1936, p. 206.

is any relation between the modern style and that shrinking of private wealth which may characterize our century, it can only be due to a deep-rooted "Zeitgeist" expressing itself in art as well as in economics'.[41] Arguing thirty years later that the modernist orthodoxy should still be followed in every detail,[42] his outlook seemed to have reached a moment of historical contradiction, for the wheel of progress had come to a halt, resting for all time on the plateau of the Modern Movement: a methodological conflict which he never resolved or probably even acknowledged. Egalitarian social engineering was a necessary condition for the victory of Pevsnerian modernism in architecture. Indeed, in *An Enquiry into Industrial Art in England* (1937), Pevsner saw as coterminous 'the levelling up of class contrasts . . . [and] the raising of standards of design'. Concern about the damaging effects of class on design was central to the argument of this book which even had a section called 'The Upper Class and Period Design'.[43] Describing 'the attitude which the socially conscious critic ought to adopt to-day' – and by 'socially conscious' he meant someone who had escaped from class – Pevsner went so far as to state, 'If the painter is not so great as to express with the utmost intensity and vitality the essence of his time, let him starve, unless he is willing to find the way back to serving the community'.[44] Here we are unhappily reminded of the enforced banishment of poets from Plato's Republic where, according to Karl Popper, began the long tradition which culminated in the totalitarian ideologies of the twentieth century. Indeed, Pevsner's desire to see the overthrow of traditional human and artistic values recalls Plato's wish to recreate a new world, free of all ugliness, both aesthetic and moral since the two are identified with each other. At the start, Plato argues, a *tabula rasa* must be created:

---

[41] Nikolaus Pevsner, *An Enquiry into Industrial Art in England*, Cambridge 1937, p. 18.
[42] *The Listener*, lxxvi, 1966, p. 953.
[43] Nikolaus Pevsner, *An Enquiry into Industrial Art in England*, Cambridge 1937, pp. 206–9.
[44] *Ibid.*, p. 198.

The first thing our artists must do – and it is not easy – is to wipe the slate of human society and human habits clean. For our philosophic artists differ at once from all others in being unwilling to start work on an individual or a city, or draw out laws, until they are given, or have made themselves, a clean canvas . . . After that the first step will be to sketch in the outline of the social system.[45]

In a parallel grim passage Pevsner remarked, 'Granted that this new style often looks rather forbidding and seems to lack human warmth. But is not the same true of contemporary life? Here, too, amenities to which we have been used are being replaced by something more exacting and more elementary.'[46]

The philosophy of progress in art, going back to Vasari and leading to the excessive admiration for the avant-garde, coloured the nineteenth century and reached a climax in the artistic manifestoes of the early twentieth century. These hailed the new dawn accompanying the birth of 'modern man' in the sort of neo-Hegelian rhetoric typified by Eckart von Sydow in a pamphlet of 1920 on *German Expressionist Culture and Painting* in which he claimed that 'We may say with but a few qualifications that the German Spirit has once more found immediate contact with the World Soul, as in the days of the Middle Ages.'[47]

Similarly, Walter Gropius looked forward in 1923 to 'the time when these isolated groups [of Modernists] will be fused once more by an all embracing and vigorous spiritual vision which must [*sic*] eventually achieve its manifestation in a great *Gesamtkunstwerk*, combining all the arts. This great communal creation, this cathedral, of the future, will in its turn illuminate with its radiance even the smallest objects of everyday life.'[48] The linking of architectural to social change was emphasized in Gropius' bold claim that 'The

---

[45] Plato, *Republic*, 501a.

[46] Nikolaus Pevsner, *An Outline of European Architecture*, Harmondsworth 1942, p. 147.

[47] Gombrich, *op. cit.*, p. 68.

[48] *Ibid.*

ethical necessity of the new architecture can no longer be called in doubt.'[49]

Frank Lloyd Wright (1869–1959) was another architect who saw himself in the role of one of Hegel's 'business managers of the World Spirit' for whom changes of styles constitute a revelation of higher, even divine, purposes. Like the architect Claude-Nicolas Ledoux (1736–1806) in his Utopian ideal town of Chaux, published in 1804,[50] Wright saw his role as that of prophet and genius, expressing his ambition for reforming the world in the same rhapsodic hortatory prose as Ledoux. Enemies of the traditional pattern of urban life such as Ledoux, Corbusier and Frank Lloyd Wright, desire the destruction of the city precisely because it is the most poignant and tangible demonstration of the frailties and strengths of the human condition. Abolishing, like Ledoux, the traditional city, Wright proclaimed that, 'The new city will be nowhere, yet everywhere. Broadacre City.'[51] For him, traditional classical architecture had to be abandoned as unethical: 'the old order has become betrayal, immoral because of the hyper-artificiality called the Renaissance or "rebirth" of the ancient order.'[52] As an example of this immorality, he cited the chain tied round Michelangelo's dome of St Peter's to strengthen it, though elsewhere he rejoiced in the tensile steel rods buried inside modern concrete. Pugin, who had convinced himself that Gothic art was Christian art and that there must be a necessary connection between religious truth and architectural truth, similarly condemned Wren's St Paul's Cathedral.[53]

---

[49] W. Gropius, *The New Architecture and the Bauhaus*, trans. M. Shand, London 1935, p. 80.

[50] C.-N. Ledoux, *L'architecture considérée sous le rapport de l'art, des moeurs, et de la législation*, Paris 1804.

[51] F.L. Wright, *An Autobiography*, London 1955, p. 282.

[52] *Ibid.*, p. 296.

[53] A.W.N. Pugin, *The True Principles of Pointed or Christian Architecture*, London 1841, pp. 4 and 8. As often, Pugin simply took to an extreme the rationalist theory of eighteenth-century French writers such as Michel de Frémin, *Mémoires critiques d'architecture contenans l'idée de la vraye et de la fausse architecture*, Paris 1702 (repr. Farnborough 1967).

The rhetoric which Wright seemed to think was necessary to justify his so-called Organic architecture was based on an appropriation of the concept of democracy. 'We are an ethically confused but still morally strong and simple-hearted people,' he claimed, 'a people that will yet instinctively bring forth a strong and healthy art when ethics and a true philosophy take hold.'[54] This is the myth of Wright's so-called 'Prairie houses': that they are unsophisticated ethical statements of American democracy because they grow inevitably out of their setting to which they are intimately attached. In fact each is an extremely expensive and beautiful work of art of great aesthetic sophistication, an aggressive virtuoso performance which is liable to be indifferent to its neighbours and setting. In a chapter significantly called 'Integrity: In a House as in an Individual' in his book, *The Natural House*, Wright claimed that 'an irresponsible, flashy, pretentious or dishonest individual would never be happy in such a house as we now call organic because of this quality of integrity.'[55] Wright evidently believed that a bad man could not be happy in a good house. Here is a confusion between art and ethics akin to that of Pugin who believed that only a good man, i.e. a Catholic, could produce good, i.e. Gothic, architecture. This brings me to the final aspect of what I objected to about the ethical or religious aspect of the defence of modernism: the claim that it is essentially truthful. Frank Lloyd Wright, for example, regretted that Americans had not been true to their innate democratic spirit and had allowed classical architecture to take hold on their soil. The result was untruth, so that Wright claimed that before his time, 'the typical American dwelling . . . *lied* about everything. It had no sense of Unity at all nor any such sense of space as should belong to a free man among a free people in a free country.'[56]

It has frequently been claimed that to express the spirit of the modern age, the construction and decoration of buildings must represent some kind of truth. In establishing what it can mean to

---

[54] Wright, *op. cit.*, p. 293.

[55] F.L. Wright, *The Natural House*, New York 1954, p. 130.

[56] *Ibid.*, p. 125.

describe architecture as 'honest', which is a favourite claim of modernists, we should be aware that, if Vitruvius is right, the whole Doric order is a fake as it is an echo in stone of techniques derived from, and properly unique to, carpentry. We should also recall that architecture is properly the art of problem solving to which concealment may be as significant as revelation. It is often forgotten that much of the built work of Alberti in the fifteenth century consisted in the partial transformation of existing buildings: his Tempio Malatestiana, Rimini, was a shell to encase the old church of S. Francesco; at the Palazzo Rucellai, Florence, his facade was a separate project unrelated to the interiors which had been built by others before his arrival; and at S. Maria Novella, Florence, he again contributed merely a facade, incorporating one partially executed in c. 1300 as part of a Gothic church, the nave of which he did not alter. Hanging like a giant piece of ornamental embroidery,[57] his work at S. Maria Novella, if it were built today, would be condemned as both untruthful and 'pastiche', not in keeping with its age, for Alberti based it stylistically on a much earlier building, the twelfth-century church of S. Miniato al Monte. One of the most admired and famous buildings of the Renaissance, Palladio's basilica at Vicenza (1549–80), also turns out to be a casing melded into an existing mediaeval structure of totally different style, materials, and configuration. Wren's St Paul's Cathedral similarly exhibits at every turn the art of concealment, of untruth.

In this context we should note the opposition of Walter Gropius to the unsuccessful campaign to preserve from demolition in 1963–5 one of the great masterpieces of twentieth-century New York, Pennsylvania Station (1902–11), by McKim, Mead and White. Gropius complained in 1968,

> Why, for instance, do we dissipate our strength by fighting battles for the resurrection or preservation of structures which were monuments to a particularly insignificant period in American architectural history, a period which . . . created what I call a 'slip-cover civilization' . . .?

---

[57] See Roger Scruton, *The Aesthetics of Architecture*, London 1979, p. 40.

Pennsylvania Station in New York is such a case of pseudotradition
. . . only a throwback to the empty mannerism inspired by the dependence of the American businessman on European prototypes.[58]

Yet architectural theorists and historians, coloured by the modernist belief that to be truthful the facade of a building must be the
'honest expression' of its interior,[59] have forgotten the disparity
between the actual floor level and the apparent floor level as implied
on the façades of Wren's Fountain Court, Hampton Court Palace,
and Trinity College Library, Cambridge. They have also underes-
timated the role of the architect as a conjuror who is called on to
transform existing buildings: for example, the facades of
Michelangelo's Palazzo del Senatore and, to a lesser extent, Palazzo
dei Conservatori, on the Capitol in Rome, are facings, or 'slip-
covers' in Gropius' condemnatory phrase, to existing structures;
Inigo Jones' remodelling of old St Paul's Cathedral in 1625–40 was
a classical skin to the mediaeval body; Adam's Syon House
(1762–9), Nash's Brighton Pavilion (1815–22), and Schinkel's
Berlin palaces as well as his most perfect work, Schloss
Charlottenhof at Potsdam, all of the 1820s, were magical transfor-
mations of existing buildings; while most remarkably, Soane was
obliged in 1822 to fit his Law Courts between the mediaeval but-
tresses of Westminster Hall which thus arbitrarily dictated the size
and proportions of what were, nonetheless, some of the most
inventive interiors in the nineteenth century.

Related to this is the element of fantasy and myth in architecture which is forbidden by the essentially joyless interpretation of
architecture as truth. A happy example of myth is the creation in
Florida in the 1920s by Addison Mizner (1872–1933) of the town
of Palm Beach and the partially completed city of Boca Raton.[60]
Mizner's public, private, and commercial buildings, designed in

---

[58] Gropius, *Apollo in the Democracy*, p. 98.

[59] See Jonathan Richards, *Facadism*, London and New York 1994.

[60] See Donald Curl, *Mizner's Florida: American Resort Architecture*, Cambridge,
Mass., and London 1984.

lively reminiscence of the historic forms of Spain, Latin America, and Italy, create an enchanting environment which brings a fourth dimension to urbanism: a created sense of history, involving the fictional patina of age and of the passage of time.[61]

The reconstruction and restoration of Colonial Williamsburg from 1927–60 through the patronage of John D. Rockefeller, Junior, would now be outlawed by the modernistic rhetoric which has been increasingly adopted by bodies such as English Heritage. Their 'philosophy' would condemn the new Williamsburg for involving 'replication', based on 'insufficient historical evidence', leading to 'unauthentic pastiche'. Certainly, about 80 per cent is new, the Capitol based on little more evidence than a single engraving, yet the whole is beautiful and highly successful. It has become part of the American psyche and a contribution to the American understanding of its past which stimulated some of the best buildings of the colonial revival of the 1930s and 40s.

We have now reached a point at the end of this Prologue where we have seen how the representation of architecture as truth has had a repressive effect on its practice. This is an appropriate moment to turn to the text of the book in which I first enlarged on this and related topics.

---

[61] It is characteristic of the dismissal of such work that there is no reference to Mizner whatever in major reference works such as the *Macmillan Dictionary of Art*, 34 vols, 1996.

Morality and Architecture

There was furious debate as to the validity of the modern movement, tempers were heated and discussion was intense. Some staff resigned and a few students went off to other schools; at any rate I was left with a deep conviction of the moral rightness of the new architecture.

James Stirling on the Liverpool School of Architecture in 1945–50 in *Buildings and Projects 1950–1974*, 1975, p. 14.

. . . nothing dates people more than the standards from which they have chosen to react.

Anthony Powell, *The Valley of Bones*, 1964, p. 158.

Prefatory Note

This book grew out of a lecture which I first gave at Cambridge in 1968 to undergraduates reading History of Art. In teaching undergraduates from 1964 onwards I had been struck by the similarities in mode of argument and criteria of judgement between the writings of Pugin and Pevsner despite the different aims they proposed. The institution by Michael Jaffé in 1968 of a Tripos paper called 'Approaches to the History of Art' gave me an opportunity to develop this line of thought, since the paper was concerned not with works of art but with what people had said, or thought they could say, about them and how the different things they said were as much coloured by accidents of time and place as the works of art themselves.

The book also owes something to a historical tradition established in Peterhouse with the publication of Sir Herbert Butterfield's *The Whig Interpretation of History* in 1931 and maintained in the college ever since. Butterfield's aim was to expose the underlying assumption by which 'the whig historian sometimes seems to believe that there is an unfolding logic in history, a logic which is on the side of the whigs and which makes them appear as co-operators with progress itself' (pp. 41–2). Though partly inspired by a desire to delineate this whig or 'historicist' outlook in certain architectural writers, the present book still remains to some extent a single lecture with the limitations that implies: that is to say it develops a single theme and is in no sense a general history of nineteenth- or twentieth-century architectural history and theory. This brings me to the point I most want to emphasize: that as the book is not a general history of the architectural thought of the period,

3

so it is not a comprehensive assessment of any of the individual critics concerned. The writings of many of the scholars discussed in the book have variety, richness, and a vast range of insights from which we can continually profit, so that when I criticize one aspect of their achievement it is with no wish to raise questions about the value of the whole but merely to contribute to a discussion of one theme in the study of architecture. Of no one over the past century is this more true than Professor Sir Nikolaus Pevsner. With his prodigious learning, energy, and enthusiasm for his subject he has been more successful than any critic since Ruskin in opening the reluctant eyes of Englishmen to works of art. Moreover, his almost incredible achievement in initiating and completing the *Buildings of England* series has made it possible for Englishmen of all types to understand and appreciate their architectural inheritance to an extent that would have been thought inconceivable before the war. All this is not in doubt and our debt of gratitude can never be adequately expressed. Without wishing to question the value of that achievement – of which, as a former pupil of Professor Pevsner, I have been a fortunate beneficiary – I would like to feel free to examine one of its postulates.

Finally, I would like to thank my friends inside and outside Peterhouse, in particular Professor Edward Shils, for helping me in writing this book.

Peterhouse, Cambridge, 1975   D.J.W.

Introduction

Exactly a century separates the publication of Pugin's *Contrasts* in 1836 from Pevsner's *Pioneers of the Modern Movement* in 1936. With a similar crusading tone each book argued for the adoption of a form of architecture not widely popular in England at the time of writing: Gothic in Pugin's case, International Modern in Pevsner's. Yet, despite the great difference between these two types of architecture, both critics use the same kind of argument to champion the cause of their chosen type: that it is not just a style but a rational way of building evolved inevitably in response to the needs of what society really is or ought to be, and to question its forms is certainly anti-social and probably immoral. In the present book, therefore, we shall outline the development in architectural writing since the eighteenth century of a tradition of ignoring the mysterious origins and the importance of 'style' and of explaining architecture away as a consequence or manifestation of something else. This 'something else' will be what happens to interest the particular critic most: religion, politics, sociology, philosophy, rationalism, technology, German theories of space or of the spirit of the age. The line of development from Pugin to Pevsner will be traced, taking in such writers as Viollet-le-Duc, Lethaby, Le Corbusier, and Giedion. Particular attention will be paid to Professor Sir Nikolaus Pevsner because his works are the richest in the corpus of architectural literature in recent times.

We shall not propose that architecture should be interpreted and judged solely in terms of visual style nor that that is the way in which it was interpreted until the eighteenth century. The idea that architecture is basically generated as a response to practical demands

was common to ancient and to medieval philosophers, as was discussion about the connection between the good, the beautiful, and
the moral. But in the numinous vision of the universe developed
by Plato and Aquinas, architecture was essentially peripheral. The
extreme mechanistic and moral justifications of architectural form
associated particularly with Viollet-le-Duc and with Pugin, to look
no further for the moment, form a theoretical tradition which is
scarcely supported by any interpretation of architecture found in
Plato or Aquinas. This theoretical tradition is sometimes supposed
to justify the forms of modern architecture, yet if those forms are
to be justified – and it probably does not matter for the moment
whether they are or not – then that justification would have
nothing to do with the supposed 'theory of modern architecture'
because there is no such theory, or at any rate none that has not
been used to justify totally different styles of architecture during the
past two centuries. What is often overlooked is that from Plato to
Choisy there existed architectural traditions, mainly Classical or
Gothic, so strong that successive debates about style were generally
contained within them. Thus the solely rational or technical explanations of architecture were subordinated to that antecedent
picture of what architecture would look like, so that their inadequacies never became apparent. Without this antecedent picture
such explanations destroy architecture and lead only to hut-
worship.[†] This is made perfectly clear by the writings of the greatest theorist of neo-Classical architecture in the eighteenth century,
Laugier, whose mechanistic and primitivist interpretation led him
to establish the hut of primitive man as the ideal and normative
type of building. However, because Laugier lived in an age which,
whatever fantasies it indulged, did not ultimately question the
supremacy of the Classical style or of Antiquity as the norm, his
simplistic and destructive theories were necessarily rendered harm-
less. Instead, they played a role in creating a stylistic transformation
from Baroque to neo-Classical within an existing Classical tradition

---

[†] See J. Rykwert, *On Adam's House in Paradise*, Museum of Modern Art, New
York, 1968.

– the 'classical language of architecture' in Summerson's phrase – which Laugier accepted as the norm almost unconsciously. The same is true of Pugin who said the same things about Gothic that Laugier had said about Classical architecture. In fact Pugin knew before he formulated his theories what he wanted architecture to look like. If one did not know that what Pugin happened to be defending was Gothic architecture one would certainly not guess from his supposed principles. How, for example, can his austere doctrine that 'there should be no features about a building which are not necessary for convenience, construction, or propriety'[1] be supposed to justify the spire of Salisbury Cathedral and not the portico of St. Martin-in-the-Fields? The way the doctrine collapses when applied to real buildings of imaginative quality has never been sufficiently emphasized and it has consequently been used to sell modern architecture to an audience prepared to believe that there is only one logical solution to the problems presented to an architect by each new commission. In fact there are a hundred and one solutions, and the one adopted will always depend partly on the current fashionable notions of what buildings ought to look like.

Three of the most persistent explanations of architecture – in terms of (1) religion, sociology, or politics; (2) the spirit of the age; and (3) a rational or technological justification – can be seen as respectively English, German, and French in origin. It is not, of course, always easy or possible to separate them. Moreover, pervading many of these approaches is a romantic and collectivist populism which believes that the architect has no imagination or will of his own but is merely the 'expression' of the 'collective unconscious'. We shall find this theme in the writings of Lethaby and Herbert Read. With Pugin, though all three approaches are present, the first is manifestly the most important. A frenzied and sometimes confused convert to Roman Catholicism, Pugin claimed in *Contrasts* (1836) the same doctrinal justification for the forms of church architecture as for the truths of the Church's teachings. It was a unique heresy which the Church might well have condemned had she thought about it.

In fact long before he became a Catholic Pugin had evidently established, solely on grounds of aesthetic taste, that Gothic was the perfect style, but in his writings he obscures that point and implies that he selected Gothic because it was the embodiment of Catholic doctrine and structural rationality. It is clear, however, that like the rational approach of Viollet-le-Duc and others, Pugin's approach does not begin to explain and justify the forms of Gothic architecture. The Catholic Church, regarding herself as the permanent exponent of revealed truth, can claim that her members believe essentially the same doctrines in 1977 as in 1477, though their implications may in the meantime have been more fully developed and understood. Yet the forms of church architecture of the two periods are totally different. In other words, the differences cannot be explained away in terms of truths or doctrines which believers must regard as permanent and unchanging.

The religious interpretation is not fashionable today, but one consequence of it certainly is. This is the belief that architecture expresses social, moral, and philosophical conditions, and that if one knows enough about such conditions in a given period one can therefore predict what its architecture will be and declare what it should be. This view can be seen in some ways as the legacy of Winckelmann and, ironically, strongly coloured the work of Pugin. It sees architecture as an instrument for the attainment of social policy employed to achieve supposedly 'moral' ends. Thus for Giedion 'contemporary architecture takes its start in a *moral* problem . . . [and where it] has been allowed to provide a new setting for contemporary life, this new setting has acted in turn upon the life from which it springs. The new atmosphere has led to change and development in the conceptions of the people who live in it.'[2]

The notion that one could argue whether architecture might actually be 'true' in the sense that one could debate the truth of religious doctrines is another legacy of Pugin's which has been of far-reaching consequence. If architecture is seen as something that can be truthful it must be immoral for it to tell a lie, and this belief runs through the French rationalists and the English Arts and Crafts

8

theorists to twentieth-century propagandists. Viollet-le-Duc, Morris, Berlage, Frank Lloyd Wright, Le Corbusier have all believed that their work was generated by truth to materials. Yet even when they used the same materials they always worked in completely different and immediately distinguishable styles. The idea that what distinguished one object from another is not style but morality has been very clearly stated by Pevsner who argued that 'sham materials and sham technique' are 'immoral'.[3]

The second of our interpretations of architecture is as an expression of the spirit of the age. Like the first, this sees the determinants of style and the criteria for assessing architectural style as lying outside architecture. It is particularly strong in the German-Swiss art-historical tradition from Burckhardt and Wölfflin to Giedion and Pevsner. To criticize some of the results of this tradition is not, of course, to deny that all history is necessarily selective and that the art historian must therefore have some organizing principle, some antecedent idea, before he approaches a particular period. This may simply be a keen ability to perceive common aims, visual and spiritual, in apparently dissimilar objects or achievements. At some moments these common aims and themes will seem so dominant in so wide a variety of media and fields of intellectual and social activities that we can reasonably speak of a spirit of the age, though this may only mean that men were more swayed by fashion then than at other times. Indeed, it may be impossible to write interesting art history without taking into account the extent to which fashions sometimes become so popular that they can dominate the mood of an age. However, art historians have often turned this tool of delicate inquiry into a crude bludgeoning weapon to be used against individual personalities in a process of making generalizations about the inevitability of particular changes. But we simply do not know why men become anxious to follow different fashions at different times. We do know, however, that since our personalities are highly complex, the reasons can only be equally complex: they will range from the trivial to the profound and some of them will be unconscious. We know, too, that our inclination to enjoy a thing precedes any attempt to rationalize or defend that enjoyment.[†] This chronology should therefore be taken into account in any interpretation of such rationalizations or defences.

The ease with which the cultural historian can distort or abuse his sense for the mood of an age is illustrated in the view expressed by Read that to him between the wars 'it seemed elementary that a belief in Marx should be accompanied by a belief in, say, Cézanne; and that the development of art since Cézanne should interest the completely revolutionary mind as much as the development of socialist theory since Proudhon.' For Read

> the cause of the arts is the cause of revolution. Every reason – historical, economic, and psychological – points to the fact that art is only healthy in a communal type of society, where within one organic consciousness all modes of life, all senses and all faculties, function freely and harmoniously. We in England have suffered the severest form of capitalist exploitation . . . We have no taste because we have no freedom; we have no freedom because we have no faith in our common humanity.[4]

Read's argument is that the *Zeitgeist*, the 'one organic consciousness', inherent in a cohesive collectivist society will inevitably express itself in 'healthy' art, the whole forming an indissoluble unity as it makes steady progress towards the complete fulfilment of the revolutionary ideal. However, although we know or think we know what themes, techniques, and materials men chose to adopt and to reject in the various historical periods we study, we must not in every case conclude that it was all a reflection of the inevitable progress of an all-pervasive spirit, a development which could not have been other than it was without upsetting the march of history. This brings us close to what Sir Herbert Butterfield

---

[†] As E.H. Gombrich argues, 'Apologists for certain kinds of art often plead that if we would only understand it, we would also like it. By and large, I think, the sequence is inverted. Without first liking a game, a style, a genre, or a medium we are hardly able to absorb its conventions well enough to discriminate and understand.' (*Art History and the Social Sciences*, Oxford, 1975, p. 51.)

called 'the whig interpretation of history' and what Sir Karl Popper described in the following words as 'historicism': 'Historicism is out to find The Path on which mankind is destined to walk; it is out to discover The Clue to History.'[5] It is the combination of this aim with a fervent belief in the *Zeitgeist* which is responsible for the line taken by many historians of modern architecture. The historian of modern culture, who believes that if a *Zeitgeist* does not exist it ought to be created, will inevitably ignore or condemn those who question what are, or what he believes ought to be, the current orthodoxies. In this way even the general public has been persuaded that it ought to believe that certain current modes, whether it likes them or not, have an authority and an inevitability which it would be improper to question. A consequence of this view in the field of architecture is expressed succinctly and characteristically by Pevsner when he writes of Marshall Sisson's substantial rebuilding of Okeover Hall in the 1950s that 'to add neo-Georgian to real Georgian' is an act the need for which 'one must be permitted to deny'.[6] But what can it mean to imply that it is 'real' for Lord Burlington to look back to Palladio but not for Sisson to look back to Vanbrugh? This denuding of the artist of all cultural resonances, of all possibility of a tradition of his own, derives from a historicist and *Zeitgeist*-inspired belief that human nature has changed radically, that a new man has been born who must either learn to express himself in a radically new way which is externally dictated by economic and political conditions, or must himself be changed radically in order to conform to these new conditions. But according to an older belief, human nature does not alter from generation to generation. Moreover, artists develop traditions which are capable of interpretation and development by other artists. It is these facts which make possible the survival and development of tradition in a culture, though the forms adopted will have different meanings for different people at different times, and possibly also at the same time since individuals may differ as much from other individuals living at the same time as they do from those living at other times.

What we have called the historicist and *Zeitgeist*-inspired historian will tend to regard modern collectivist ideas as right; he will be ever anxious to deal wholesale with 'humanity', to label individuals as types, to identify them in classes, and to seek for total consistency throughout all fields of intellectual, social, and spiritual activity. He believes in a state which is antagonistic to all groupings which come between it and the individual and which will allow no real power or autonomy to any subordinate structures, ranging from the family to the corporation. He expects to find in the past the same total consistency with a single overriding principle or pattern which he thinks political organization is trying to establish in the present. But if we begin to concentrate our attention on the individual we will know from looking into ourselves that this supposed consistency with a dominant pattern, easy enough to believe in when we are concentrating on theoretically constructed types, simply does not exist in fact. Nevertheless, this direction of attention away from the individual and from the particular traditions of the various arts with which the individual artist interacts, has been a powerful influence on the assumptions which underly much twentieth-century art history. These assumptions echo in varying degrees Alois Riegl's notion of *Kunstwollen* which implies that the will of the individual is powerless against the *telos* of art and that it is not the artist but art that 'wills'. Professor E.H. Gombrich has drawn attention to the history of this tradition in art-historical writings, but less notice has been taken of the history of architectural history.

The third of the three interpretations which we have identified is the rational or technological.[†] From at least the eighteenth century, French critics, whether proposing Classical, Gothic, or 'modern' architecture, have generally argued that it was or should be the natural outcome of a rational intellectual discipline applied to the solution of measurable practical or technological problems. The inadequacy of this view may be instanced by the vault of a Gothic church where the details may be rationally worked out in themselves but are essentially a means to an end which cannot be

---

[†] See E.R. de Zurko, *Origins of Functionalist Theory*, Columbia U.P., 1957.

rationally justified since the real roof to the church is the lead and timber roof visible from outside though not from inside. The kind of imaginative leap involved in the decision to have an elaborately ornamented stone vault at all cannot be ignored when we describe how Gothic buildings came into being or when we draw up a programme for a present-day architecture. The mechanistic interpretation of Gothic is particularly associated with Viollet-le-Duc who summarized it when he wrote: 'There are in architecture – if I may thus express myself – two indispensable modes in which truth must be adhered to. We must be true in respect of the programme, and true in respect of the constructive processes.'[7] Here is the beginning of what we might call the 'programme-worship' of modern architectural theorists who believe that the elaborate specifications which the modern client, often a public body, hands to architects and engineers in the form of a 'programme' will and should dictate their own architectural solution. Sir John Summerson, a particular admirer of Viollet-le-Duc, has generally maintained too sophisticated and independent a stand to ally himself to the cause of the crusade we shall be investigating in the present book. None the less, his published lecture of 1957, 'The Case for a Theory of Modern Architecture', was pre-occupied with the search for a 'source of unity' in twentieth-century architecture and proposed that 'the programme as the source of unity is, so far as I can see, the one new principle involved in modern architecture . . . It is part of my case for a theory of modern architecture that it is the source.'[8][†]

Significantly, the inadequacy of this view was exposed by a historian, Reyner Banham, and by an architect, Peter Smithson, in the discussion which followed Summerson's lecture. Banham pointed out that

---

[†] Summerson subsequently withdrew from this position and wrote of his R.I.B.A. lecture of 1957: 'I had to give the paper – I had committed myself and it was duly printed, but that was the moment at which I stopped being an architectural propagandist and, indeed, an architectural critic at all'. (*Architectural Association Journal*, lxxv, Feb. 1960, p. 151.)

when Gropius was thinking about the Bauhaus teaching programme he thought of it in terms of neat rectangular rooms or drew rectangles and circles connected by long straight lines, like the circulation diagram of a Hertfordshire school. Once you started to think about the programme of the building you were committed to a set of symbolic forms.

Smithson put the same fundamental point in a more general way:

> To say that you can evolve a form from a social programme or from an analysis of the situation in terms of flow and so on is meaningless, because analysis without the formal content, the architect's particular specialisation, has one factor missing from it.

The comments of Banham and Smithson go some way to demolishing what we have called the morally insinuating and widely disseminated argument that modern architecture exercises some special unassailable claim over us since it is not a 'style' which we are free to like or dislike as we choose, but is the expression of some unchallengeable 'need' or requirement inherent in the twentieth century with which we must conform. This frequently repeated argument is wholly arbitrary: those who propose it construct first of all a picture of twentieth-century society to which they then impute 'needs' and as a result demand that architecture must conform with those needs. The technique is succinctly expressed in Pevsner's threatening assertion that 'unless a further levelling of social differences takes place in this country, no steady development towards the aims of the Modern Movement is possible.'[9] But the 'needs', of course, are the invention of the critics who speak of them. They are needs only in so far as they are needed to realize the beliefs associated with a particular political or social programme which could only be imposed by a party but which may by no means be widely shared. Even if they were widely shared they would have no necessary moral standing and certainly no proper authority over art and architecture. This technological, mechanistic, and political approach has affinities with the two approaches we have already defined: those of morality and of the spirit of the age. In this third approach we are again faced with the imposition of a criterion external to architectural style itself. In this case it is an arbitrarily chosen technological, political, or social 'necessity'.

Programme-worship and the technological approach have recently gained new support from those whose approach to architecture cannot but suggest that the forms of architecture can be generated by mathematical modelling and the use of the computer. The implication here is that all human desires can be discerned by statistical, sociological, and psychological surveys and can be expressed numerically so that, as one modern critic has put it, 'architecture is the system of controls on which the arrangement of the urban scene is based'.[10] The inadequacy of this as an explanation of the forms of modern architecture can easily be shown in a building which, ironically, is elevated to key status in Reyner Banham's *The Architecture of the Well-tempered Environment*, 1969. This is the Royal Victoria Hospital in Belfast of 1903, a neglected pioneer in the introduction of air-conditioning. But the point we should note is that the sophisticated system of air conditioning was conceived as part of a building designed in a wholly traditional Victorian style. In other words, the presence of advanced technology need not determine the form of the building which contains it. The architect can certainly decide that he wants his building to look like a building that contains advanced technology, but that is an aesthetic decision which we should be free to accept or reject as we wish. None the less, the old views die hard. Sir Leslie Martin was still able to argue, in a paper called 'Architects' approach to Architecture' published in the *R.I.B.A. Journal* in 1967, that modern architecture rested 'on an important shift of attention and process' that took place in the 1920s and 1930s and from which 'three powerful lines of thought appeared'. These he defined as follows:

The first came from the passionately held belief that there had to be some kind of complete and systematic re-examination of human needs and that, as a result of this, not only the form of buildings, but the total environment would be changed. The second line of thought, interlocking with this, was simply that change in the form of buildings, or environment, would only be achieved completely through the full use of modern technology. These two ideas produced a third, which was that each architectural problem should be constantly reassessed and thought out afresh.[11]

The so-called 'human needs' are defined arbitrarily, arrogantly, and with a complete disregard for the importance of tradition as a guide to the architect. The article was accompanied by illustrations depicting the realization of these principles in the form of Martin's scheme for the 'development' of Whitehall, first published in 1965 as *Whitehall: a Plan for a National and Government Centre*. These proposals, which were subsequently dropped by a Labour government, involved the elimination of numerous buildings of interest throughout a vast area both in and near Whitehall from the smallest shop to the largest public building. The large-scale destruction, socially and architecturally, of a historic environment in favour of the creation of a 'national centre', illustrates clearly the dangers attendant upon the assumption by architects that they have some special social mission allegedly based on a 'complete and systematic re-examination of human needs' so as to 'change the total environment'. However, Martin attached so much significance to the principles of the Whitehall scheme that he set up a research group at the Cambridge School of Architecture where they could be developed and extended. This was known, significantly, as the 'Centre for Land Use and Built Form Studies', a title which indicated clearly enough a belief that architecture as an art involving taste, imagination, and scholarship should finally be abolished and replaced by a scientifically plotted Utopia in which tamed collectivist man with all his wants defined by technology and gratified by computerized planning would contentedly take his apportioned place as in some gigantic rationalistically constructed beehive.†

---

† For a fuller account of the work of this 'Centre', see R. Scruton, 'The Architecture of Stalinism', *Cambridge Review*, vol. xcix, 16 Nov. 1976, pp. 36–41.

What is ignored in most of the interpretations we have so far out-lined is that architecture is an art with its own traditions, and not a science, so that its concern with image-making[12] is at least no less vital than its solution of practical problems. Thus, as Mark Girouard put it, modern architecture 'has failed almost completely, for instance, to produce images of enjoyment or entertainment, or images of domesticity with which any large number of people can identify'.[13] Moreover, ideas on what is or is not practical and con-venient vary so much from one individual, country, and time to another that an architecture devised solely as a 'communal service' based on the fulfilment of 'practical requirements' defined by archi-tectural and academic doctrinaires, might ultimately be found more unpractical than one which gave stress to other considerations. An analogy with costume, an important subject largely neglected by art historians, may be helpful here. Like architecture, costume might be supposed by some to fulfil a basically practical role, yet, like the architect, the costume designer must create an image with which the public wishes to identify and it is perhaps surprising how little the public is concerned with what planners would deem practical. An unhappy example of this in costume would be the craze for 'platform shoes'; a happy example in architecture would be the Palladian villa in early eighteenth-century England which led Alexander Pope to comment wryly that modern patrons were 'Proud to catch cold at a Venetian door'.[14]

But since the mid-eighteenth century there has developed a con-spiracy of silence about the truth contained in Pope's penetrating observation. Historians and theorists have ignored that, whatever else it may do, architecture cannot escape involvement with image-making. Instead, they have been searching 'for an ideological base which would remove architecture once and for all from the arena of Style and fashion',[15] a base from which they could propose ruth-lessly rationalistic and collectivist solutions to 'the whole question of the relationship of the total environment to community need'.[16] Pevsner believed that the final solution of this question had been reached with the International Modern movement and that any deviation from it would be anti-social and immoral. This quasi-religious commitment to a secular ideal acquires a particular emphasis in men who have abandoned formal religious belief themselves or who, like Pugin, have temporarily confused religion with architecture. Pugin argued that what he was defending was 'not a *style*, but a *principle*',[17] and that pathetic fallacy is echoed again and again in the nineteenth and twentieth centuries by men anxious to cling to some objectively existing truth in a godless world. Thus Ruskin wrote of the Renaissance that 'it is not the form of this architecture against which I would plead. . . . But it is the moral nature of it which is corrupt';[18] and even today Stirling, hero of the architectural *avant-garde*, can write of his student days at Liverpool School of Architecture in 1945–50: 'There was furious debate as to the validity of the modern movement, tempers were heated and discussion was intense. . . . At any rate I was left with a deep conviction of the moral rightness of the new architecture.'[19] The architect Marcel Breuer similarly claimed that 'to us clarity means the definite expression of the purpose of a building and the sincere expression of its structure. One can regard this sincerity as a sort of moral duty . . .'[20]

For Lethaby, as earlier for Viollet-le-Duc, the Gothic cathedral 'was not designed as beauty, it was developed along a line of experiment as surely as the great ocean liners were developed';[21] indeed, in his view 'a noble architecture is not a thing of will, of design, of scholarship'.[22] This particular torch was kept burning by Le Corbusier and handed on to Giedion who also asserts – indeed rather suspiciously over-asserts – the belief that 'there is a word we should refrain from using to describe contemporary architecture – "style". The moment we fence architecture within a notion of "style" we open the door to a formalistic approach. The contemporary movement is not a style . . .'[23] Finally, Pevsner stated the view in an extreme form when he attacked all European architecture from 1760 to 1860 on the grounds that like Art Nouveau it consisted merely of surface fashion, and that because 'it is based on individual inventiveness, a genuine universal style could not therefore spring from it.'[24] One of the developments we shall be tracing in the following pages is the consequence of the belief that modern man should build a new collectivistic society based on a universally accepted moral and social consensus in which architecture would be an unassailably 'genuine' and 'universal' truth no longer marred by the 'individual' and 'inventive' traits of the old world in which individual taste and imagination were regarded as important.

*. . . dissoluta terrestris hujus incolatus domo, aeterna in coelis habitatio
comparatur.*

Roman Missal, Preface for the Dead.

PART I

The Theme in the Nineteenth Century

1. Pugin

The central argument of Pugin's *Contrasts* (1836) is that there is a necessary connection between religious truth and architectural truth. The reasoning which enabled him to state this argument with such confidence can be reconstructed in the following way: as a Catholic convert he was naturally impressed with the Church's divine teaching authority, her insistence on her role as the sole exponent of revealed truth, and, quite improperly, he sought to extend that teaching *magisterium* to areas outside divine revelation. Disliking Classical architecture for a variety of emotional, associational, and aesthetic reasons, and noticing that its adoption in this country more or less coincided with the Reformation, he came to regard it as a consequence of the Reformation; and since the Reformation was morally reprehensible so must be its architecture. The supposition on which Pugin and his followers based so much is fundamentally false because the Church has in fact no infallible teaching to give her flock concerning the desirability of one architectural style rather than another, any more than she teaches that there is one divinely appointed system of political government. To argue, as Pugin does, that the arts employed by the Church to symbolize her divine truths are themselves somehow infused with the aura of unchanging truth is a curious materialist heresy. A characteristic example of his exaggerated language occurs in the course of an attack on the design of modern vestments and the custom of hiring outside choirs to sing at Mass:

Since Christ himself hung abandoned and bleeding on the Cross of Calvary, never has so sad a spectacle been exhibited to the afflicted Christian as is presented in many modern Catholic chapels, where the adorable Victim is offered up by the Priests of God's Church, disguised in miserable dresses intended for the sacred vestments . . . [accompanied by] the performances of an infidel troop of mercenary musicians . . .[1]

The belief that people would actually be better and nicer if surrounded by Gothic detail rather than Classical is central to the illustrations in *Contrasts*. For example, in the views of 'Contrasted Public Conduits', modern Classical and ancient Gothic, the handle of the modern pump is padlocked and a stern policeman carrying a truncheon orders away a child who has come with his jug, whereas the Gothic conduit is in perfect working order. This kind of irresponsible fantasy, entertaining though it is, suggests the unreality of Pugin's position.

In short, Pugin wrote about art and architecture as though they were part of a religion. This approach has been echoed by the many nineteenth- and twentieth-century critics who have written about all manner of subjects as though they were religion: for example, Gropius who argued that 'the ethical necessity of the New Architecture can no longer be called in doubt',[2] and Leavis who seems to regard the moral standards of a society as somehow emanating from literature and literary criticism, from the 'collaborative creativity'[3] of the modern university. All of these could point to the precedent of Pugin when they suggest that the cultural style they are defending is an inescapable necessity which we ignore at our peril and that to support it is a stern ethical and social duty.

The weakness of Pugin's argument is further exemplified in his bitter attack on the Georgianization of medieval church interiors.[4] To us today the incorporation of Georgian panelling and box-pews can lend a real appeal to a dull medieval church of no special architectural interest. We know, moreover, that had the churches remained in Catholic hands they would have been subjected to a more complete Classical transformation in the seventeenth and eighteenth centuries than they underwent at the hands of Anglicans.

Contrasts is simply an attack on the Reformation and on its supposed debasement not only of the architecture of its day but also of the general taste of Pugin's own day. It is also a plea for a return to Gothic as the only way to cure the ills of the Reformation. His next book, *The True Principles of Pointed or Christian Architecture* (1841), can be seen as an attempt to make out a rather different case for the revival of Gothic in order to convince those who were unmoved by the anti-Protestant argument. What this meant in practice was bringing in the theories of French rationalism which had been the stock-in-trade of architectural theorists in France and Italy for a century and a half, during which time they had been used to justify a variety of styles. In his *Essai sur l'architecture* (1753) and *Observations sur l'architecture* (1765), the influential Laugier had encapsulated the tradition of defining architectural beauty in terms of structural honesty. However, as we saw in the Introduction, he was sufficiently a man of the eighteenth century to incorporate his new articles of faith – function and utility – into the old religion of the Classical tradition. To an English audience, unfamiliar with the arguments worked over by Perrault, Cordemoy, Frézier, Blondel, Laugier, Lodoli, and the rest, this mechanistic interpretation had an irresistible air of novelty and authority. The one fundamental contribution made by Pugin was the carrying over from *Contrasts* of the notion that architectural truth was conterminous with religious truth. This notion is implied in the very title of the new book, 'Pointed or Christian Architecture', and confirmed early on when he writes: 'Indeed, if we view pointed architecture in its true light as Christian art, as the faith itself *is perfect, so are the principles on which it is founded*'.[5]

If pointed architecture is perfect truth then it must not tell a lie; it must not seem to be what it is not. Thus Pugin writes: 'Now the severity of Christian architecture is opposed to all deception. We should never make a building erected to God appear better than it really is by artificial means.'[6] Pugin's refusal to recognize the fact that *a building is by its very nature artificial* derives from his belief that since Gothic architecture is divinely ordained it is not marked by human imperfections but is an inescapable reality. Subsequent generations of critics, up to the present day, who certainly have not attributed divine authority to any particular style, nevertheless have gone on believing in the possibility of a way of building that was not artificial, not marked by human imperfections, and that represented some inescapable reality. Of course Pugin himself was not really committed for a moment to the full implications of that French rationalism which lies behind his claim in *True Principles* that we should not use 'artificial' means to make buildings look better than they are in 'reality'. Indeed, later in the same book he flatly contradicts himself when he writes: 'One of the great arts of architecture is to render a building more vast and lofty in appearance than it is in reality.'[7] Pugin loved Gothic: he loved the Catholic Church: he decided that the one was the permanent embodiment of the other. Here, indeed, was pure function raised to the level of religious truth. Yet critics have taken his espousal of functionalism at face value and out of context. Professor Phoebe Stanton published an article in 1954 called 'Pugin: Principles of Design *versus* Revivalism' which implies that, driven by a need to find a rational system of building construction, he hit on Gothic as the perfect answer.[8] In fact the development of his mind was the reverse of this. Driven by a passionate love of Gothic he seized on any and every argument which might be used to justify its revival, though the argument from religious truth and from functional or technological necessity took precedence over any aesthetic arguments.

One of the arguments he hit on was based not in rationalism but in nationalism. This was fraught with consequences for the nineteenth and twentieth centuries. He argued that in consequence of the deplorable stylistic variety of late neo-Classical architecture with its Greek, Roman, and even Oriental revivals, 'national feelings and national architecture are at so low an ebb, that it becomes an absolute duty in every Englishman to attempt their revival'.[9] It is one of the curiosities of the history of taste to find an architect, half a Frenchman, arguing for the adoption of a style of French origin as part of a recovery of nationalist feeling in England.

Elsewhere he stated that 'the erection of the Parliament Houses in the national style is by far the greatest advance that has yet been gained in the right direction'.[10] This nationalist argument also shows the arbitrariness of those who justify aesthetic choices by extraneous arguments.

Although in espousing the cause of nationalism he felt obliged to condemn Regency Picturesque, elsewhere he upholds the doctrines of the late Picturesque theorists and offers them as though he had discovered them himself. Thus, echoing the writings of Price and Knight, he declares:

> *The picturesque effect of the ancient buildings results from the ingenious methods by which the old builders overcame local and constructive difficulties.* An edifice which is arranged with the principal view of looking picturesque is sure to resemble an artificial waterfall or a made-up rock, which are generally so *unnaturally natural* as to appear ridiculous.
>
> An architect should exhibit his skill by turning the difficulties which occur in raising an elevation from *a convenient plan* into so many picturesque beauties . . . But all these [modern] inconsistencies have arisen from this great error, – *the plans of buildings are designed to suit the elevation, instead of the elevation being made subservient to the plan.*[11]

But arguments like these can mean whatever one wants them to mean, can be used to defend or attack whatever one has decided one likes or dislikes. Though Pugin borrowed them from the theorists of the Picturesque, he would not allow that they justified Picturesque architecture. The way in which Nash allowed all manner of accidents to influence the form and layout of his Regent Street and Regent's Park development, rather than imposing a symmetrical intellectual scheme, is today acknowledged as a triumph of Picturesque planning. All Pugin could see, however, were 'those nests of monstrosities, the Regent's Park and Regent Street, where all kinds of styles are jumbled together to make up a mass'.[12]

Two years after *True Principles* came another similar work, *An Apology for the Revival of Christian Architecture in England* (1843). By this time Pugin does not have to explain in his title that Christian means Gothic, so confident is he of the success of his earlier propaganda. He does feel obliged to explain why, if Gothic is the permanent and divinely appointed style for Christians, it 'was not developed till several centuries after the crucifixion of our Lord'.[13] Needless to say he can offer no explanation that will satisfy anyone who has not already decided for quite other reasons that Gothic is the best style. Similarly, he feels that something is required of him concerning the applicability of Gothic to new building requirements such as railway stations. He illustrates its suitability by contrasting two drawings of railway bridges sporting Gothic arches and mouldings, with two drawings based on the despised Euston Station, one of which shows in a lamentably crude and inaccurate fashion the celebrated Greek Doric entrance gateway. Even the trains respond to the 'improved' architecture: while the engine at Euston disfigures the station with clouds of smoke and steam, an engine in the Gothic station allows itself no more than a few Picturesque puffs. Even if it be granted that in the nineteenth century Gothic enjoyed some special appropriateness or 'propriety' for church design, it is hard to see on what grounds it could enjoy the same appropriateness for railway architecture. In fact the only possible justification for using it was that Pugin liked the Gothic style best and could not be satisfied until everything was made to conform to that. M.R. James understood the mentality when he made the Verger in 'An Episode of Cathedral History' lament the destruction of Georgian woodwork in the choir of Southminster Cathedral with the words: 'But Dean Burscough he was very set on the Gothic period, and nothing would serve him but everything must be made agreeable to that.'[14]

That the bold and dramatic Euston Arch, so much admired today, was a particular *bête noire* to Pugin serves to emphasize that his theory of 'convenience, construction, or propriety' means only what the individual decides it is going to mean. Thus, while Pugin would justify a spire on the grounds that it had a symbolical function or purpose, he would not allow that the great propylaeum at Euston similarly fulfilled a symbolical role: for him it was no more than 'a striking proof of the utter disregard paid by architects to the *purposes* of the building they are called upon to design'.[15]

We have argued that Pugin's writings lent support to those who believed in 'a way of building that was not artificial, not marked by human imperfections and that represented some inescapable reality'. Pugin hints at such an architecture when he states that 'a pointed building is a *natural building*', and that 'I trust, before long, to produce a treatise on *Natural Architecture*'.[16] In such a treatise we would doubtless have been told frequently that 'every building that is treated naturally without disguise or concealment cannot fail to look well',[17] though we could be equally certain that we would never be allowed to stray far from Pugin's belief 'that the beauty of architectural design depended on its being the expression of what the building required, and that for Christians that expression could only be correctly given by the medium of pointed architecture'. This notion of a natural architecture, so inevitable that its forms should not be open to question, has long outlasted the belief that it had already been achieved in Gothic. Pugin's mode of argument adumbrated the tendency which has been widespread since his time to deny or falsify the role of aesthetic motivation and to claim instead guidance from considerations of 'naturalness', utility, functional advantage, and social, moral, and political necessity, or simply from correspondence with the 'spirit of the age'.

2. *Viollet-le-Duc*

'Should anyone attempt to construct a theory of modern architecture in harmony with the conditions of thought prevailing today, he will discover no starting point so firm, no background so solid as that provided by Eugène Viollet-le-Duc.'[18] So Summerson wrote in 1949 in the first of two essays which argued that with all their strengths and weaknesses Viollet-le-Duc's writings were the basis of modern architecture. The essence of Viollet's *Dictionnaire raisonné de l'architecture française du XIe au XVIe siècle* (ten volumes, 1854–61) was that he took it for granted that every feature of Gothic architecture had a functional or technological origin and justification. He derived this from the French tradition of rationalist architectural theory from Cordemoy† to Rondelet, which we have referred to elsewhere, and used it to justify propaganda for a new nineteenth-century architecture that would be based on a scientific exposition of Gothic. These principles were given clearer and more readable exposition in the two volumes of his *Entretiens sur l'architecture* published from 1858 to 1872. On the first page of Volume I the vital question is asked, what are the social conditions under which art best flourishes, 'Is man in becoming civilized, refined, tolerant, moderate in his tastes, and well-informed, – such in fact as our social conditions can make him, – thereby rendered more apt and capable in the domain of Art?' The answer is a resounding 'No': 'Philosophy, gentle manners, justice, and politeness constitute a state of society in which it is agreeable to live; but this state may be unfavourable to the development of Art.'[19]

He therefore concludes that 'the value of art is independent of the element in which it originates and flourishes', and that to estimate the value of art which may have been 'highly developed and perfected under a very imperfect civilization' we must adopt 'laws which belong exclusively to the Arts, and are independent of the state of civilization to which nations may attain'.[20] This calm and lucid approach, so French in its air of detachment, is very different from German *Kulturgeschichte* and from the 'social commitment' of twentieth-century architects and their defenders. So why does Summerson imply that Viollet-le-Duc will somehow be found to be 'in harmony with the conditions of thought prevailing today'? The answer is that once he gets into the body of his book Viollet soon drops his quiet detached air and it becomes clear that he has a very determined view of the only kind of society which can produce good art: it is secular, egalitarian, rationalist, and progressive. Moreover, he begins to rely on a belief in the *Zeitgeist* to

---

† See R.D. Middleton, 'The Abbé de Cordemoy and the Graeco-Gothic Ideal: a Prelude to Romantic Classicism', *Journal of the Warburg and Courtauld Institutes*, xxv, 1962, pp. 278–320, and xxvi, 1963, pp. 90–123.

explain away his dislike of Roman and eighteenth-century architecture as expressions of social orders of which he could not approve. This lands him in difficulties with Gothic architecture which he is forced to explain not as an expression of the feudal and monastic *Zeitgeist* but as an attack on it.

As a great force for good in society, architecture is too serious to have anything to do with style or 'the caprices of that fantastical queen we call Fashion; [for] when it becomes the plaything of a people without fixed ideas or convictions, and when no longer reflecting national Manners and Customs, it is but an encumbrance, – a thing of mere curiosity or luxury'.[21] Once the Queen of Fashion with her wayward individual tastes has been deposed, Viollet-le-Duc will be there ready to set up the republic of fixed ideas. For him everything must be reducible to, and explicable in terms of, reason. Consequently for him, 'style depends only on the application to an object of the reasoning faculty',[22] and all buildings are good if they show evidence of rationalist composition, bad if they do not. To illustrate the second volume of the *Entretiens* he designed a number of painfully hamfisted examples of rationalist construction involving blunt conjunctions of load-bearing iron and masonry assembled with no object other than that of seeming to fulfil measurable functional and technological requirements. There has been general agreement that, though interesting as intellectual exercises, these are thoroughly unattractive in every other way, thus disproving Viollet's belief that a well-reasoned and practically useful design must always be an aesthetically successful design. Moreover, the designs are structurally misconceived and are an early example of mock-engineering.

Viollet-le-Duc seems in certain passages to be one of those writers who see only two possible alternatives for architecture: either as capricious fashion, arbitrary and trivial, or as the expression of some external centre of gravity such as social and political ideals, technological necessity, or the spirit of the age. To those who adhere to this outlook, the existence of an artistic tradition with its own canons of judgement and its own standards does not occur.

Viollet's ideas about architecture derive in general as well as in three important particulars, from eighteenth-century neo-Classicism: he has, first, an underlying Romantic faith in the truth and morality of Greek architecture and society which derives from Winckelmann and which was also developed by Marx who saw the essential quality and appeal of Greek culture as a reflection of the childhood of the human race;[†] secondly, a related 'primitivist' notion that Roman and Renaissance architecture lost contact with the pure fount of Greek truth, and is thus morally and stylistically in questionable taste; and, thirdly, a belief, deriving from the rationalist theorists of eighteenth-century France, that beneath the appearance of Gothic architecture there must lie some constructional system capable of universal application so that if only it could be isolated and defined it could serve as the key to all our present problems. For him Greeks and Goths link hands across a sea of troubles: 'the Greek arts are free and independent, the Roman arts are enthralled; and if the barriers placed between the two camps, ancient and modern, were thrown down, there is every reason to believe that the Greek artists would have a much more cordial understanding with those of the Middle Ages than with the Romans, who have been ranked as their allies, while in reality they are only their oppressors.'[23] Trying to define the nature of this enthralment, he writes: 'one of the characteristics of Architectural Art at the close of the seventeenth and during the eighteenth century is the absence of style',[24] and again: 'the style of Architecture during the declining years of the Roman Empire and that of the eighteenth century consist [sic] in the absence of style'.[25] The reason for this is that they all 'show an evident contempt for the form really appropriate to the object and its uses'. Thus, 'if a Roman matron of the period of the Republic were to appear in a drawing-room filled with ladies dressed in hooped skirts with powdered hair and a superstructure of plumes or flowers, the Roman lady would present a singular figure; but it is none the less certain that her dress would have *style*, while those of the ladies in hooped

---

[†] For a discussion of this point see E.H. Gombrich's excellent booklet, *Art History and the Social Sciences*, Oxford, 1975, p. 24.

skirts would be in (the style of the period), but would not possess *style*.'[26] Similarly, modern Classical architecture is 'a sin against taste, for taste consists essentially in making the appearance accord with the reality'.[27] Compared with modern Classical architecture even ancient Roman begins to look truthful:

> A Roman-Corinthian monolithic isolated column of marble or granite has style, because the eye, ascending this huge block of stone from base to summit without perceiving a single joint, comprehends its rigid function, which is perfectly indicated by the material and its homogeneity. But a Corinthian column composed of courses of stone, like those of the Madeleine, or the Pantheon in Paris, has not style, because the eye is disquieted at seeing such slender points of support formed of small stones piled one on the other.[28]

So the eighteenth-century column, like the hooped dress, is a sin against 'taste' because its outward appearance does not correspond with what its constructional reality is in the case of the dress, or ought to be in that of the column. The implication seems to be that technological function and materials left to their own devices will somehow suggest the form, so that the less man interferes in the process, with his imagination and caprice, the better. Gothic art is continually held up as a shining example of this *laissez-faire* materialism: Viollet writes of thirteenth-century architecture, 'in this general movement individualities soon disappeared, and architecture assumed the form of a science'.[29] In this anonymous process of assembly no one will have to exercise the power of choice since everything can safely be left to the dictates of the 'programme': 'There are in architecture – if I may thus express myself – two indispensable modes in which truth must be adhered to. We must be true in respect of the programme, and true in respect of the constructive processes.'[30]

As we have already argued in the case of Pugin, this kind of language either means nothing at all, or is demonstrably wrong as when, for example, it leads Viollet to condemn columns made up of drums rather than monoliths. The dreary consequences of the vain attempt to eliminate the human contribution to the art of architecture – with all the suppression of memory, taste, imagination, and tradition that this implies – are clearly spelt out towards the beginning of the final chapter of the first volume:

> In the study of the arts of the past, therefore, we should observe a clear distinction between a form which is only the reflection of a tradition, a form adopted without consideration, – and a form which is the immediate expression of a requirement, of a certain social condition; and it is only the study of the latter that issues in practical advantage, – an advantage not consisting in the imitation of this form, but in the example it affords of the application of a principle.[31]

In his worldly or what might today be called his 'consumer-oriented' materialism, it did not occur to him either that the 'reflection of a tradition' might itself be the 'immediate expression of a requirement' which was more binding than a mechanical requirement, or that forms of which the motivation is primarily aesthetic can appear to be the consequence of technological necessity. Thus a persistent tradition in modern architecture, from the glazed staircases of Gropius's Werkbund building of 1914 to Stirling's glazed History Faculty building at Cambridge of 1964, has been the belief that glass has some special and unchallengeable role as the expression of the spirit of modernity. In fact its use is generally an aesthetic urge disguised as a technological necessity and in the History Faculty, for example, certainly cannot be justified by 'convenience, construction, or propriety'. Thus without some antecedent aesthetic idea, no amount of faith that the 'programme' or the materials will somehow suggest their own solution will be capable of producing architecture.

As we mentioned earlier, Viollet-le-Duc has in fact a very clear picture of the only type of society which can produce good architecture, although there is a sense in which he pretends that he has not. He could not reconcile his picture of Gothic architecture as a truthful rational structure evolving inevitably from simple faith in programme and materials, with his knowledge that its builders had believed in God and authority and lived in a feudal society that was inegalitarian and therefore, to him, irrational or untruthful. If Gothic architecture was just a natural way of building, the first thing Viollet had to do was to remove from it any suspicion of association with priests and particularly with monks, since if it is unnatural to be a priest it is still more so to be a monk. He did this by drawing a contrast between Romanesque and Gothic. Romanesque already stood condemned because it looked back to Roman art, the art of thraldom and oppression; it could now be further condemned as an art produced by monks:

> We have an art that sprang from Roman traditions and Byzantine influences, – Romanesque art cultivated in the cloisters; in a few years we quit this for a new phase of art, practised exclusively by laymen – an art based on geometry and the observation of laws hitherto unknown – the equilibrium of forces; and this art continually advances; it soon transcends its original aim. The lower classes combine and obtain privileges by force or address; we become merchants, agriculturalists, and manufacturers.[32]

The tendency to make of history a mirror wherein we see our own reflection could hardly be more clearly demonstrated than in Viollet's picture of a Gothic world closely resembling the developments of nineteenth-century European society. In his false antithesis between Romanesque and Gothic, he conveniently forgets on the one hand the great strength of the Romanesque tradition in secular architecture and, on the other, that Suger, the patron of the first Gothic building, was a Benedictine monk. The note of fantasy, or at least of wishful thinking, which colours his interpretation of the relationship between Gothic design and Gothic society, is persistently maintained and developed. He writes of the origins of Gothic:

> The Encyclopaedic spirit, and the application of the exact sciences engaged the attention of enlightened men; and the influence of the monks then disappeared for ever from the history of art. Architecture fell into the hands of laymen . . . The desire for political consolidation

and union, the tendency to investigation, to the acquisition of knowledge, and to the immediate practical application of what had been
acquired, and the reaction against religious corporations were dis-
tinctly expressed by the architecture: men reasoned on every question
that presented itself; they examined everything; they had a firm belief
in the progress of science, and exhibited a daring boldness without
pausing a single day in their rapid career. In this general movement
individualities soon disappeared, and architecture assumed the form
of a science.[33]

The interpretation of Gothic as lay, bourgeois, secular, almost
Protestant, is probably inspired by the writings of the scholar-
statesman, F.-P.-G. Guizot (1787–1874).[†] To Viollet's fertile mind
the curious notion now suggested itself that this great body of
laymen must have felt the need to agitate for political 'rights' like
nineteenth-century workers, and that the cathedrals were somehow
an attempt to sublimate those desires:

We must not forget that architecture was then cultivated only by
laymen belonging to the common people, having under them guilds
of craftsmen. It would seem that the middle class of society . . . felt
the necessity of association . . . which should render it, so to speak,
independent of the past, and allow it to follow an entirely new path.
This class of artists and craftsmen, not being able to claim political
rights, and not hoping to rival the power of the feudal noblesse, strove
for enfranchisement by work; they made architecture a kind of free-
masonry, to which initiation was requisite – an initiation that was
constantly made more difficult: this middle class felt that they possessed no material vantage-ground, – that study and the practice of
the arts could alone secure them a moral independence . . . For the
rise of that architecture was but the awakening of the ancient Gallic
spirit: a spirit which . . . forced a way to light and liberty through
every available issue. Gothic architecture, at its commencement, was
a protest against monastic influence . . . its stones speak; they do not

---

[†] I owe this suggestion to Dr. Robin Middleton.

express 'suffering', as we were recently told by the *Académie des Beaux Arts*, but, on the contrary, enfranchised labour, – the triumph of an intellect which feels its power, which acts, which is asserting its independence, while ironically concealing its secrets from blind or indifferent masters, and which is conscious that it will one day become in its turn the ruling power.[34]

Elsewhere we are told that 'in the thirteenth century the art invented by the secular school was essentially democratic',[35] and that today we can recapture that spirit 'in spite of three centuries of oppression'; thus 'in our own times, as in all former periods, it is from below that the movement proceeds . . . the old spirit of the lay craftsmen of the twelfth century is being gradually awakened, for in France the humblest workman reasons and desires to understand what he is doing; and he conceives a passion for works in whose general plan as well as in the details he can detect a logical sequence. Our workmen are, in fact, of the same stuff as our soldiers . . .'[36]

It need hardly be pointed out that it is all a fantasy world of Viollet-le-Duc's own creation, and that a different and more realistic picture of the Gothic world has emerged from the patient researches of scholars ranging from Emile Mâle in 1910 to John Harvey in the present day.

Finally, we may observe in Viollet's writings how his belief in democracy and in the *Zeitgeist* led him to argue that phases in architectural development are produced collectively and from the bottom upwards. The unlikely thesis that 'it is from below that the movement proceeds' was developed in a book published near the end of his life, *L'Art russe, ses origines, ses éléments constituifs, son apogée, son avenir* (1877), where he wrote:

It is never from above that those invigorating principles emerge without which art degenerates into imitation; it is from below, it is through the popular consciousness or instinct. Every renewal is the consequence of something worked out in the spirit of the people, of the masses: it is never the product of an élite.[37]

It is characteristic of the populist democrat that he locates the *Zeitgeist* in the *Volk* or *le peuple*: sociologism and Hegelian historicism are combined here, as they are in Marxism. Yet it would be wrong to suggest that we have painted in this chapter a full or balanced portrait of Viollet-le-Duc, or indeed that we have painted a portrait of him at all. We are concerned only to show the ways in which a particular theme has affected the approaches of different writers and scholars at different times.

. . . the revolution will be brought about by the proletariat, and will not be imposed on it from above by an enlightened section of the middle classes. The progressive section of the middle classes can most usefully collaborate by arousing the proletariat to political consciousness and organising it for the struggle. In the same way the culture of the revolution will be evolved by the proletariat and not imposed on it from above by the enlightened middle classes.

Anthony Blunt, 'Art under Capitalism and Socialism',
The Mind in Chains: Socialism and the Cultural Revolution,
ed. Cecil Day Lewis, 1937, p. 114.

The general election of 1945 showed what had happened. Suddenly in the full (and very cold) light of peace it was seen that the war had also been a revolution; that in the course of it a social fabric had been steadily and remorselessly, and with general consent, demolished, and that it now only remained to sort out the wreckage and rebuild. . . . 1945–51 was something much more than a vigorous convalescence. It altered irrevocably the national meaning of architecture.

J. Summerson, Introduction to T. Dannatt,
Modern Architecture in Britain, 1959, p. 19.

PART II

The Theme in the Twentieth Century

1. Lethaby

The doctrine of Viollet-le-Duc lies behind the writings of the influential critic, architect, and educator William Richard Lethaby (1857–1931). A pleasingly eccentric product of the English Arts and Crafts movement overlaid with French rationalism, his views have been taken very seriously by successive propagandists of modern architecture beginning with Pevsner in *Industrial Art* (1937). For J.M. (now Sir James) Richards he was in 1940 'the wisest of all English architectural writers',[1] and Macleod, who described him in 1971 as 'my central figure', proclaimed that 'I now feel for him something akin to his own "uncritical admiration and reverence" which he expressed for Philip Webb'.[2]

Lethaby's best-known book is probably *Architecture, an Introduction to the History and Theory of the Art of Building,* first published in 1911 in the 'Home University Library of Modern Knowledge' and reaching a wider audience in subsequent editions between the wars. From the point of view of the theme we are trying to trace in the present book, Lethaby's most telling arguments are that Gothic was just a natural way of building which evolved inevitably out of the technology of construction and materials, and that the Renaissance was reprehensible because it involved knowledge, taste, and connoisseurship. The picture he gives of Gothic is as follows:

. . . a Gothic cathedral may be compared to a great cargo-ship which has to attain to a balance between speed and safety. The church and

39

the ship were both designed in the same way by a slow perfecting of parts . . . Nothing great or true in building seems to have been invented in the sense of wilfully designed . . .

A noble building, indeed any work of art, is not the product of an act of design by some individual genius, it is the outcome of ages of experiment. . . . Thus it was that a cathedral was not designed, but discovered, or 'revealed'. Indeed building has been found out – like speech, writing, the use of metals – hence a noble architecture is not a thing of will, of design, of scholarship. A true architecture is the discovery of the nature of things in building . . .[3]

It would be hard to devise a more misleading interpretation of Gothic. Inherently improbable in the face of the sparkling grace and imagination everywhere present in Gothic art, which can only have been the product of individual personalities with will and taste, it is an interpretation which has been entirely demolished by modern scholarship. Thus George Henderson writes: 'we cannot suppose that the mediaeval artist was any less capable, exacting, or professional, than his more self-conscious successors in later centuries',[†][4] and John Harvey in publishing a series of medieval 'Texts on Style and Fashion' writes of 'the false assumption that educated men of the period simply accepted style and changing fashions heedlessly. Many texts prove the contrary: changes were keenly observed, and in particular the great change from Romanesque to Gothic'.[5] Typical of the texts he cites is that referring to the rebuilding of Auxerre Cathedral in 1215 by the Bishop of Auxerre:

'The Bishop saw that his cathedral at Auxerre was an old building and very small, suffering from decay and age, while others in every direction round about were raising their heads in a wonderfully beautiful style (*mira specie venustatis*) . . . He had it pulled to the ground . . . that,

---

[†] See in particular Henderson's entertaining contrast between Blake's romantic depiction of a wild uncouth Gothic artist, the personification of peasant toil, and the reality as represented in a highly sophisticated medieval portrait of Hugues Libergier, a genuine Gothic architect.

putting off the decrepitude of antiquity, it might grow young in a more elegant style of novelty.'[6]

Such passages as these are particularly valuable for demolishing Lethaby's Romantic populist interpretation of Gothic development as a slow evolution scarcely noticeable whilst in progress and not likely to be much affected by the whim or taste of individuals. In fact what is striking about Gothic is the suddenness of its arrival at Saint-Denis in 1140, and the speed with which it was imitated and developed in the Great Ile de France cathedrals.

Having established to his satisfaction that Gothic architecture was not the product of 'will, design and scholarship', it was inevitable that he should attack Renaissance architecture which so clearly was. It is dismissed in the surprisingly short space of barely eight pages, which makes the four chapters devoted to Egyptian and Babylonian architecture seem somewhat excessive by contrast. He reluctantly admits that because of the survival of Roman buildings in Italy, 'The Renaissance in Roman Italy was . . . a perfectly natural impulse, and was, indeed, inevitable', but believes that it cannot be justified outside Italy. 'Perhaps', he muses, 'if it had taken some different turning it might have been more obviously beneficial . . . In looking back, art loses its life'.[7] He is very anxious to show that the Renaissance does not, and cannot, have life:

the Roman revival as a whole has proved arid and sterile, nothing grows from it . . . It must, I think, be admitted by those who have in part understood the great primary styles, Greek or Gothic, that the Renaissance is a style of boredom. However beautiful single works may be, it tends to be blind, puffy, and big-wiggy . . . Its highest inspiration was good taste, it was architect's architecture. Splendid works were wrought even in the age of its gloomy maturity by Peruzzi, Michael Angelo, and Wren, but as a whole it seems to be the art of an age of Indigestion . . . the Renaissance as a whole lacked the spirit of life. Gothic art witnesses to a nation in training, hunters, craftsmen, athletes; the Renaissance is the art of scholars, courtiers, and the connoisseurship of middlemen.[8]

The attack on 'architect's architecture' springs from the belief we have been investigating that architectural works are always determined by extra-architectural criteria. The juxtaposition of scholars and athletes is simply the reflection of Lethaby's Romantic, anti-intellectual populism. The fantasy and real hatred which run through his account hardly need to be indicated. Particularly offensive is the refusal to take Renaissance architecture seriously and the consequent lapse into a homespun critical language, e.g. 'puffy, and big-wiggy', in contrast with what is allegedly expressive of the 'reality' of the people. The Renaissance is condemned by a false contrast with the Middle Ages in which, remarkably, there were supposed to be no architects, scholars, or courtiers: whereas as Henderson writes:

> The age of the Renaissance was to inherit from the Middle Ages the ideal of the omnicompetent artist, able to plan and devise all aspects of some great enterprise, ready to turn his hand to half-a-dozen tasks . . . Then again Leonardo helps us to realise that no very violent revolution has taken place in the economics of art and the status of the artist as we move from the Middle Ages into the age of the Renaissance.[9]

Lethaby's collectivist and anti-intellectual view of European architecture – an idiosyncratic blend of the Arts and Crafts movement and Viollet-le-Duc – could be regarded as part of a search 'for an ideological base which would remove architecture once and for all from the arena of style and fashion'. With this chimera in mind, Lethaby was ready to define what modern architecture must be. In 1920 he wrote: 'We require an active art of building which will take its "style" for granted, as does naval architecture';[10] and in *Architecture* he argued: 'All modern buildings have too much that is merely capricious. Little in ancient architecture was "designed". Things designed by a single mind are mostly "sports", which must quickly perish. Only that which is in the line of development can persist.'[11] The final message of the book is that in the consensus on which this architecture of collective endeavour will be established, 'the only agreement that seems possible is agreement on a scientific basis, on an endeavour after perfect structural efficiency'.[12] The trouble is, of course, that structural efficiency is only a means and not an end. In itself it is not particularly interesting except to the specialist or the structural engineer, just as the detailed workings of the human organs are generally of interest only to the physiologist and the doctor. Most people take structural efficiency for granted, and surely should be allowed to do so. It will only obtrude itself if it goes wrong, just as we only become preoccupied with the functioning of our bodily organs when they go wrong. Without wishing to build too much on this biological analogy, one could argue that with man and architecture structural efficiency is of value and interest only as a means to an end.

The passages we have been quoting represent an interesting combination of Romantic collectivism (i.e. *Volksgeist*) and functional necessity. The Romantic populist view, developed in the early nineteenth century, was that the anonymous people, labouring silently in confrontation with the hard tasks of life, produce works which no one has deliberately designed but which are products of the unconscious wisdom, the adaptive resourcefulness, of the 'folk-soul'. This idea seems to pervade several of the interpretations of architecture we are investigating in the present book: for example, the religious and social determination, and the argument from technological necessity. It also relates to the all-pervasive collectivist belief that the architect has no will or imagination of his own but is simply the 'expression' of something lying in the 'collective unconscious'. He must ever respond to collective needs and must act as the collectivity demands.

2. Brave New World

Lethaby anticipated in many ways the Brave New World mentality of the creators of the Modern Movement and their supporters between the wars. Mies van der Rohe, for example, represents this mentality perfectly, though he overlays it with the tradition of

Kunstwollen characteristic of recent German art history. In 1923 he wrote: 'We reject all esthetic speculation, all doctrine, all formalism. Architecture is the will of an epoch translated into space; living, changing, new'; and in 1925: 'We refuse to recognise problems of form but only problems of building'.[13] In a paper of 1924 called, significantly, 'Baukunst und Zeitwille', Mies van der Rohe developed further this blend of Lethaby and the *Zeitgeist* into a menacing vision of the depersonalized, secular, mechanistic future:

> Greek temples, Roman basilicas and mediaeval cathedrals are significant to us as creations of a whole epoch rather than as works of individual architects. Who asks for the name of these builders? Of what significance are the fortuitous personalities of their creators? Such buildings are impersonal by their very nature. They are pure expressions of their time. Their true meaning is that they are symbols of their epoch . . .
>
> The whole trend of our time is towards the secular. The endeavours of the mystic will be remembered as mere episodes . . .
>
> We are concerned today with questions of a general nature. The individual is losing significance; his destiny is no longer what interests us. The decisive achievements in all fields are impersonal and their authors are for the most part unknown. They are part of the trend of our time towards anonymity.[14]

The preaching of a chosen type of architecture as an inescapable natural and moral commitment was given firm emphasis at this time in Le Corbusier's *Vers une architecture* (1923). The book consisted of a rather random republication of a number of articles in slogan form which had first appeared in the journal *L'Esprit nouveau* in 1919–22. The consequent muddle and lack of unified argument enabled readers to decide for themselves what its principal message was. They had no doubt that it was Functionalism, though in certain romantic passages Corbusier, in a very unMiesian way, had indicted its inadequacies.

The book begins with his celebrated concept of the house as 'a machine for living in',[15] a parallel to Lethaby's more homespun view that 'we must aim at getting the small house as perfect as the bicycle'.[16] Le Corbusier's argument that 'the House Machine . . . [is] healthy (and morally so too)'[17] combines succinctly the pathetic fallacies we are investigating: that particular types of architectural form are morally regenerative and physically health-giving. The transference of the principles of human morality to inanimate objects had led Pugin and Ruskin to attack the illusionism of Renaissance and Baroque architecture on the grounds that because man should not tell a lie buildings should not. Le Corbusier expresses the same fallacy at the beginning of his opening chapter when he claims that architecture is 'a question of morality; lack of truth is intolerable, we perish in untruth',[18] and we find later on that this inevitably leads him to attack the Renaissance. Like Ruskin he finds the Romanesque, by contrast, morally acceptable and he writes of the twelfth-century Santa Maria in Cosmedin in Rome: 'To think that this church was in existence in Rome when the great Renaissance was in full swing with its gilded palaces and its horrors!'[19] And there is even a page of photographs, called 'The Rome of Horrors', which includes details from the Palazzo Barberini, the Galleria Colonna and the Castel Sant 'Angelo. The old Puritan idea that simplicity is moral and elaboration immoral leads him to one of the most extreme examples of his particular version of the pathetic fallacy: the caption of a photograph of one of the Parthenon triglyphs, 'Austere profiles. Doric morality.'[20] His obsession with the notion that 'primary forms are beautiful forms because they can be clearly appreciated'[21] produces a most unexpected onslaught, not only on Renaissance but on Gothic architecture:

Gothic architecture is not, fundamentally, based on spheres, cones and cylinders. Only the nave is an expression of a simple form, but of a complex geometry of the second order (intersecting arches). *It is for that reason that a cathedral is not very beautiful* and that we search in it for compensations of a subjective kind outside plastic art.[22]

Along with the worship of simple forms goes a worship of machinery. This is carried to its extreme in the section of the book called the 'Manual of the Dwelling' where Le Corbusier claims that it is preferable to listen to mechanically reproduced music (even the pianola!) than to live music because in the latter case one has the embarrassment of actually seeing live musicians: 'The gramophone or the pianola or wireless will give you exact interpretations of first-rate music, and you avoid catching cold in the concert hall, and the frenzy of the virtuoso.'[23] Elsewhere in the 'Manual' we learn that there must always be 'gymnastic appliances' in the bathroom and that each occupant must have a dressing room. 'Never', Le Corbusier admonishes us like a Victorian nanny, 'undress in your bedroom. It is not a clean thing to do.'[24] In fact, in his celebrated Villa Savoye, Le Corbusier merged a principal bedroom into a bathroom without any real dividing wall between them. Hygiene movements had been popular in France since the turn of the century but really originated in Germany as part of the process of national rehabilitation, the 'renewal of the German people', after the defeat of Prussia in 1807. The hygiene mania of Le Corbusier was part of the general argument for purity, and seems somehow to reflect a hatred of tradition as essentially 'unnatural'. The Modern Movement combined this rationalist belief in elementary uncluttered schema with the collectivist approach based on belief in the needs of the age and in the nascent 'real' spirit of the age.

The idea, then, runs through Le Corbusier's book that what is simple, supposedly functional, and materialistic in aim, light in colour, and immediately apprehensible in form, enjoys advantages in terms of health and morality over other different or more complex solutions. Thus it must be imposed on society as soon as possible if we are to avoid revolution, and to bring this point home the last chapter is indeed called 'Architecture ou Révolution'. In fact Le Corbusier is himself 'revolutionary', inasmuch as he has an unquestioning faith in the advantages of what is called 'public ownership'.

The whole book is thus an amalgam of Pugin, Viollet-le-Duc, Choisy, Lethaby, and the rest, bound together with a certain apocalyptic fervour. It was translated into English by the architect Frederick Etchells in 1927 and has been republished frequently ever since. In an edition of 1946 the publisher wrote, 'This book has probably had as great an influence on English architectural thought as any one publication of the last fifty years.' A sobering thought.

Le Corbusier's functionalist argument and its apocalyptic overtones were taken up and exaggerated a year or so later by the German architect Bruno Taut in his book, *Modern Architecture*, 1929:

> If everything is founded on sound efficiency, this efficiency itself, or rather its utility, will form its own aesthetic law. A building must be beautiful when seen from outside if it reflects all these qualities ... The architect who achieves this task becomes a creator of an ethical and social character; the people who use the building for any purpose, will, through the structure of the house, be brought to a better behaviour in their mutual dealings and relationship with each other. Thus architecture becomes the creator of new social observances.[25]

Here we have a clearly stated Puginian view of architecture as essentially a socially manipulative force. What is less clear is the nature of this proposed new society which the forms of modern architecture are going to engender. All we know is that it will, of course, be quite different from any previous society. That Le Corbusier had also fallen victim to the fallacy that the human mind can ever become a *tabula rasa* is evident from his claim that he had designed the Villa Savoye 'pour des clients dépourvus totalement d'idées préconcues'.[26] The absence in authors such as Taut of any serious thought on the nature of the proposed new society makes the claim, that modern architects have some special socially constructive role to play and message to offer, a particularly empty one. While Taut is absolutely specific about what the new architecture is going to look like, he defines its social role – which he regards as a matter of equal urgency – in loose and vacuous language:

> Here is the beginning of a new life which will take the place of ideals which are fast dying out. And this life already has the tradition of a century behind it . . . This tradition is that of the power of production, which, according to Bernard Shaw, must always be revolutionary. According to him, every healthy thinking person must be filled with revolutionary impulses; but they can only

become real revolutionaries in later life after recognising the difficulties involved. This has not been very differently expressed by Lenin, in the words that 'all serve the Revolution whose work within their profession remains strictly objective'.[27]

Where Le Corbusier had seen architecture as a parallel to or substitute for the social revolution, Taut is more explicit about their identical roles (though anything but explicit when it comes to details). Towards the end of the book we are shown the divine light of modern architecture illuminating the way from a Ruskinian Apocalypse to the Communist Utopia:

> It has been asserted that literature and music also, to a certain extent, are now just emerging from the state of adolescence into that of manhood; that in lieu of sentimental claims, facts are now considered as authoritative and style-forming . . . The same might just as well be claimed for architecture . . . The age of manhood brings with it a state of mind in which there is not so much inclination to be led away by a beautiful idea, but rather to be concerned with real facts . . . One might almost see a connection between the synchronous erection of the Crystal Palace and the Communistic manifestos of Marx and Engels . . .
>
> This darkness of the future will terrify many . . . It is just at this point that the fecundity of modern architecture will have to pass its strongest test.[28]

In Taut, then, we see a shift from the belief in architecture as the tail wagged by the ideological dog, to architecture as a central agent in the renewal of society. The architect takes on the task of interpreting the 'needs' of society and by his constructions guides those needs to gratification in an appropriate form of society, namely 'healthy' socialism.

Five years later this new doctrine of modernity was preached by Herbert Read in *Art and Industry* (1934). It is inspired by the self-delusion we found in Le Corbusier that there is a new thing called modern man, a new animal without roots in the past and whose mind is, or must become, a *tabula rasa*. Speaking on his first page of the radically new art that will be appropriate for this new man,

48

Read argues that not until we have 'stripped it of all the irrelevancies imposed on it by a particular culture or civilisation, can we see any solution of the problem'. Man without a memory will produce art with no aim other than the immediately measurable and practical: art which meets 'real needs'. In tribute to the mechanistic theories of Viollet-le-Duc and Lethaby, Read believed that Greek and Gothic man had already achieved an architecture inspired solely by the need to fulfil man's animal needs:

> In the twelfth and thirteenth centuries, as in the fifth century B.C., there existed, in Northern Europe and in Greece respectively, phases of architectural development, and of industrial design generally, that have never been excelled in history. There is one significant fact about such periods: they are without an aesthetic. What they did, they did as the solution of practical problems, without taste, without academic tradition.[29]

It is evident in such a passage that Read's passionate commitment to the promotion of modern design has blinded him to the obvious shallowness of his arguments. The notion of cathedrals being assembled by bands of anonymous mechanics without taste or traditions is a surprising one for any twentieth-century art historian to entertain, and, as we have already shown, the researches of modern scholars should by now have suppressed any lingering affection for it.

Along with the technological interpretation of medieval art goes the inevitable attack on the Renaissance. He describes how as a consequence of the sinister growth of educated patrons with cultural expectations that were 'fed by the type of learning which the Classical Revival encouraged, there sprang up a tradition of connoisseurship or dilettantism, based on the knowledge and appreciation of such works of art. This tradition is known to us as *Taste*, or *Good Taste*, and to it, I think, we owe all the confusion of values that has existed since the sixteenth century until the present day.'[30] Like the Italian Futurists, Read is able to write off the cultural achievement of the past four centuries confident that modern technology is the Messiah for which the world has been waiting since the age of the cathedrals. Comparing a five-hundred-foot-high mast at the B.B.C. West Regional Transmitting Station with Gothic architecture, he claims that 'Gothic verticality may have evolved in exactly the same way – the engineering solution of a problem preceding the consciousness of a resulting aesthetic experience'.[31] The belief in the absolute value of adhering to the requirements of technology derives in part from a belief in the spirit of the age and that the spirit has come to reside in the machine. Popper has shown how such a preoccupation leads to a belief in the urgency of novelty and change. In Read's case all this is overlaid with a vague Marxism, a materialist determinism. Thus he writes towards the end of the book: 'The economic law is absolute, and healthy; it compels the human spirit to adapt itself to new conditions, and to be ever creating new forms. It is only when sentimentality and a nostalgia for the past are allowed to prevail, that these forms cease to evolve in conformity with aesthetic values.'[32]

In Read's *Anarchy and Order* (1954) we learn a little more about the new society and the new art: as the expression of unchallengeable truths, neither of these will any longer be 'artificial' but will be reconstituted as part of a permanent 'reality'. Read describes how the first step on the road to truth was achieved when 'painting revolted, like poetry, against the artificiality and irrelevance of the academic tradition of the eighteenth century'. These heroic pioneers were men 'whose aims and whose achievements have step by step built up a new conception of reality – a conception of reality totally opposed to the bourgeois standards of the period. Constable began a movement which includes Courbet, Daumier, Van Gogh, Cézanne, and Seurat'. Read summarizes the significance of this tradition in the following way: 'The main tradition, the only tradition which is revolutionary in essence, in its fundamental vision of life, that is the tradition which must be integrated with the social revolution.'[33]

Any attempt to unravel this tangled skein of false sociology and false art history confronts us eventually with Read's ambition of establishing in social organization as well as in artistic form an enduring and unassailably ideal 'reality'. According to this view, just as the art of Seurat, for example, is somehow 'real' and 'classless' rather than 'artificial' and 'bourgeois', so will the social revolution

establish a new order that is natural and truthful because it has been
stripped of all the false restrictions and distinctions artificially
imposed on it. This cant culminates in a picture of the ideal future:

> The inevitable is the classless society – the society without a bureau-
> cracy, without an army, without any closed grade or profession,
> without any functionless components.[†] A hierarchy of talent, a divi-
> sion of labour, there must be; but only within the functional group,
> the collective organization. Whether responsibility and efficiency
> should be rewarded is a nice problem for the future; what is certain
> is that it should not be rewarded by any kind of money or tokens of
> exchange which could give one man power to command the services
> of another outside the collective organizations. . . .
>
> In the classless society, the mind of every individual will have at
> least the opportunity to expand in breadth and depth, and culture will
> once more be the natural product of economic circumstances, as it
> was in Ancient Greece, in China, in Medieval Europe, and indeed in
> all the great epochs of civilization.[34]

In common with several of the writers we are investigating, Read
puts an emphasis on 'naturalness' and seems to interpret its meaning
as meeting 'real needs'. These 'needs' frequently spring from technological developments which, it is believed, should determine
what men ought to be or do. For Read, economic circumstances
are normative so that man's actions must be guided by them and not
guide them.

Read offered what the collectivists of the 1930s wanted to hear,
whether they were Fabian Socialists, National Socialists or, like Read
himself, Anarchist Socialists. He was undoubtedly a figure of powerful influence at this time. Along with Lenin, he is cited as an
authority by Anthony Blunt in an essay entitled 'Art under
Capitalism and Socialism.' This appeared in a collection of essays by
Marxists and fellow-travellers edited by Cecil Day Lewis under the

---

[†] Tawney criticized modern society for not being 'functionally' organized in
guilds (*The Acquisitive Society*, 1921).

title *The Mind in Chains: Socialism and the Cultural Revolution* (1937). 'In the present state of capitalism', writes Blunt, 'the position of the artist is hopeless',[35] but he looks forward to the 'real' art which will emerge from the proletarian revolution. He explains that:

> In the nineteenth century when the *bourgeoisie*, being still on the upgrade, was attempting to impose its culture on the working classes, it was impossible for artists representing these classes to attack and discredit the culture that was being offered to them. But at the present time, when the workers are in a more hopeful position, with a workers' state actually formed and a workers' culture built up in the U.S.S.R., this is no longer the most important function for the revolutionary artist.

Blunt describes for us what 'the real art of the socialist state' will be like. It will be 'alive and effective, and what it will have lost in comparison with *bourgeois* art will be a certain refinement, which is not at all necessarily a sign of living and progressive art. The new art will be less sophisticated, but more vital than the old.'[36]

It was Herbert Read who suggested to Leslie Martin the idea of writing a handbook for the general public explaining the virtues of modern domestic furniture and fittings. This appeared in 1939 as *The Flat Book*, an aptly-titled textbook illustrative of the 1930s taste for the minimal, the stackable, the washable, for what the authors called 'the contemporary demand for convenience and efficiency'.[†] Design is seen as a kind of democratic anodyne beyond the reach of time and fashion, so that in the Foreword the authors express the hope that the book will 'at least be a method of ridding ourselves of the more transient forms of "fashion value" by means of which so much furnishing is sold today'.

[†] Characteristic are the illustrations (p. 57) of the '"I.B.A." five purpose bath' which, with a white wood cover, makes 'a table for general use'; with the flap of the cover folded back, a wash basin; with the cover removed altogether, 'a home laundry including wringer'; and, with the addition of a grooved flap, a kitchen sink and draining board. It can also be used as a bath, once the wringer has been removed, though only in a sitting posture.

In 1937 Leslie Martin had been a joint editor with Ben Nicholson and Naum Gabo of a book with the curious title, *Circle International Survey of Constructive Art*. In their editorial preface the editors referred to the 'new cultural unity' which they hoped to establish. They made it clear, as Pevsner was doing in his *Enquiry into Industrial Art in England* published in the same year, that social manipulation would play an essential role in the achievement of this 'unity'. Hence their regret 'that popular taste, caste prejudice, and the dependence upon private enterprise, completely handicap the development of new ideas in art'.[37]

In the opening article Gabo attempts to explain what is meant by 'constructive' art. He believes that 'the war was only a natural consequence of a disintegration which started long ago in the depths of the previous civilization', and that the new art will be constructive in the sense of reversing that general process of disintegration. Modern science is another great force which will have its role to play in this process of regeneration. According to Gabo, the task of 'the scientists of our century . . . consists in the construction of a new stable model for our apprehension of the universe.' Thus the new constructive art will also be scientific in some sense: indeed 'at those moments in the history of culture when the creative human genius had to make a decision, the forms in which this genius manifested itself in Art and in Science were analogous'. For example, 'Raphael would never have dared to take the naturalistic image of his famous Florentine pastry-cook as a model for the "Holy Marie" if he had not belonged to the generation which was already prepared to abandon the geo-centrical theory of the universe.'[38] The generalizations about the analogies between a modern science and constructive art are not pursued and instead we are offered several pages of the empty declamation associated with modern manifestos: 'In the light of the Constructive idea the purely philosophical wondering about real and unreal is idle. Even more idle is the intention to divide the real into super-real and sub-real, into conscious reality and sub-conscious reality. The Constructive idea knows only one reality. Nothing is unreal in Art.'[39]

Other designers and theorists take up the theme in a series of short illustrated essays. From Mondrian we learn that the new constructive art will be intolerant of any competition from the past: 'Certainly the art of the past is superfluous to the new spirit and harmful to its progress: just because of its beauty it holds people back from the new conception!'[40] Nicholson informs us confidently that '"painting" and "religious experience" are the same thing. It is a question of the perpetual motion of a right idea.'[41] For Gabo, 'constructive sculpture is . . . ready to lead us into the future';[42] while Le Corbusier believes that 'the pure regenerating spirit of modern times will be expressed by organisms with a mathematical interior'. These organisms will also echo the architecture of primitive times when 'there was no decoration in the houses; people lived with a robust simplicity – proof of their moral wholesomeness'.[43] J.D. Bernal looks forward to the establishment of 'painting and sculpture which is a powerful part of the social movements of the time', and laments that at the present time 'paintings and sculptures are purchasable objects, not parts of well-conceived social construction'.[44] The concluding essay, by Lewis Mumford, is called 'The Death of the Monument'. It is a hymn of praise dedicated to the new man of the twentieth century, the godless liberated humanist:

> For the most radical change in our modern cosmos has come about through our changed conception of death and immortality: for us, death is an episode in life's renewal, the terminus of a radical maladaptation: continuity for us exists, not in the individual soul, but in the germ plasm and in the social heritage, through which we are united to all mankind and all nature: renewal comes in the sacrifice of the parent to the child, in the having lived to the living and the yet-to-live. Instead of being oriented toward death and fixity, we are oriented toward life and change.[45]

To remind ourselves, if such a reminder be necessary, of the fundamentally pernicious nature of such writing we could do no better than to quote the following passage from Sir Herbert Butterfield:

Hitler in *Mein Kampf* pointed out that nature is ruthless since she is prodigal with individual lives and considerate only for the development of the species; and because he had taken nature as his pattern or first principle, because he envisaged primarily man-in-nature (and then transferred his conclusions or his inferences to man-in-history), he regarded this inhuman principle as one which was applicable to the human race . . . Too easily we may think of man as merely the last of the animals and in this way arrive at verdicts which we are tempted to transpose into the world of human relations. And some people are so accustomed to thinking of great collectivities and handling them in a mathematical manner, that the whole human story is to them only an additional chapter in the great book of biology. On such systems as these the individual matters little – he is the foam on the wave – and the only thing to consider is the development of the species as a whole. Upon our willingness to engage ourselves rather with man-in-history depends the valuation that we place upon personality, or personalities, as such.[46]

Mumford chose to reprint 'The Death of the Monument' as part of the final chapter of his book, *The Culture of Cities* published in 1938, the year after *Circle*. Elsewhere in the same chapter he gave an even clearer indication of what he meant by society which is not centred on belief in the importance of 'the individual soul, but in the germ plasm and in the social heritage'; and of what he thinks will be the role of modern architecture in the creation of such a society:

Taken together, modern form, modern architecture, modern communities are prophetic emergents of a biotechnic[†] society: a society

---

[†] In a glossary, Mumford explains that the word 'biotechnic' refers to 'an emergent economy' in which 'the key inventions, on the mechanical side, are the airplane, the phonograph, the motion picture and modern contraceptives, all derived directly, in part, from a study of living organisms'. He goes on to observe that 'the application of bacteriology to medicine and sanitation, and of physiology to nutrition and daily regimen, are further marks of this order: parallel applications in psychology for the discipline of human behaviour in every department are plainly indicated'.

whose productive system and consumptive demands will be directed towards the maximum possible nurture, under ever more adequate material conditions, of the human group, and the maximum possible culture of the human personality. What has so far been accomplished is but a taste of the more thorough-going order that is to come. So far, architecture and community planning have aided experimentally in the clarification of this order: but further re-valuations of doctrine and belief, further accretions of positive knowledge, will in turn alter profoundly the new communities we are in process of building. Throughout the world, a consensus is gradually being established among men of good will and effective competence. Let us then attempt to seek further the social basis of modern form, and to establish even more definitely its underlying principles.[47]

Mumford's talk about the manipulation of 'the human group' by means of 'the more thorough-going order that is to come' so as to form 'new communities' which will achieve a 'consensus' about 'the social basis of modern form', gives us a clear view of the Utopia towards which Martin, Gabo, and Nicholson were leading us in *Circle* with modern design as the essential agent in the process of transformation. One of the principal missionaries in this movement was Richards, who had befriended Pevsner on his arrival in this country and had joined the staff of the *Architectural Review* in 1935. The title of his contribution to *Circle*, 'The Condition of Architecture and the Principle of Anonymity', is immediately indicative of his notion of 'the social basis of modern form'. His defence of the forms of modern architecture which he favoured consisted in extending the view of Greek and Gothic as types of anonymous collective endeavour to cover English eighteenth-century architecture as well. Nineteenth-century architecture stood condemned as an example of 'malady' and 'decay' of which the cause was 'a socio-psychological one': in other words, it lacked that 'settled anonymity in architectural design' which should have been established 'as the echo or reflection of a unity of social and cultural purpose pervading the whole of life'. The 'important quality of inevitability', which is supposed to come if one can abolish style, can be found in the eighteenth century because 'the architects, in the sense of the designers, (usually simply the builders) were anonymous – that is to say, their personalities were culturally irrelevant'.[48] This inhuman fantasy is developed as follows:

> Though the architecture of the eighteenth century was based on an imported mode, and though it was the age of that anti-social being, the talented amateur or connoisseur, it absorbed that mode into a genuine folk art: no longer imported, but the natural – the only – means of expression of genuine folk *work*. . . . this universal tradition of the eighteenth century may be regarded culturally as the continuation of the mediaeval tradition. In mediaeval times the anonymity – and the universality of the idiom – was even more characteristic. The impulse – or purpose whose unity made this tradition possible – was a religious rather than a civic one: an emotional rather than a rational.[49]

We need hardly stress the close connection here between anonymity and collectivism as cause and ideal, and the consequent suppression of the achievement of the individual imagination within the framework of an artistic tradition. In his stand for anonymity and populism and against patronage and connoisseurship, Richards reminds us immediately of Lethaby. Richards recognizes that a problem which might arise from his populistic ideal is that some people might suppose 'that we already have an anonymous folk architecture of our day: the mass-produced villas and bungalows that constitute the acres of suburbs surrounding all our towns and cities'.[50] And certainly, if one were really seeking a twentieth-century folk art, one could hardly find a more complete example than in the gnomes and half-timbered garage gables of suburban England. But, for what appear to be sociological, not artistic, reasons, Richards cannot allow that these really aspire to the condition of a true anonymous folk architecture. He thus writes of the speculative builder: 'His products *form no part of a socio-cultural whole.*' In other words, the praise of folk art turns out to be a screen behind which he can propose arguments in favour of social engineering which will create a totally integrated and consistent whole. The real reason that mass-produced villas could not constitute a genuine anonymous folk architecture is because they were part of a 'socio-cultural whole' determined by the survival of middle-class values and the private speculator. We were, after all, warned in the Editorial 'that popular taste, caste prejudice, and the dependence upon private enterprise, completely handicap the development of new ideas in art'. Richards reiterates this point when he emphasizes that 'the answer, then, to the question how we can regain a true folk architecture remains a sociological, or political one'.[51] The power-ful desire for unity, for what Richards called the 'socio-cultural whole', is closely related to the historicist belief that every period contains an all-pervasive, all-dominating theme or idea. This worship of the 'consistency' of art, technology, and social organiza-tion is part of a denigration of the dignity of artistic modes and part, too, of a tendency to make them mere expressions of something else. The emphasis which we find in Richards on the 'whole' or holism with its opposition to individual imagination is, as Popper has pointed out, characteristic of historicism.

What, then, is the society and what are the politics for which *Circle* can be seen as thinly veiled propaganda? The answer is, of course, the ideal of the progressive intellectuals and fellow-travellers of the 1930s: Soviet Communism. But Richards' views of the rela-tionship between art and politics had not prepared him for the fact that the perfect society established in Russia since 1917 had still not, in his view, produced the perfect architecture by 1937. He is pre-pared to accept, however, that there may be a certain time-lag:

That, even if the sociological side is tackled first, the cultural cannot be relied upon to readjust itself immediately is shown by the case of Russia. There, the social unity of purpose which has successfully been re-established had not yet crystallized itself into a new cultural one; art of a bourgeois nature still flourishes, partly in reaction against the extremist, revolutionary movement that tried to set up an abstract ideology with inadequate technical equipment; but largely because, owing to *psychological* instability, the superficial advertisement of

progress becomes more important than the fact of progress – sociological development has progressed so much faster than educational.[52]

Three years later Penguin Books chose to publish Richards' *An
Introduction to Modern Architecture* which had a wide popular influence both during and after the war. Richards opens his book by
lamenting the poor quality of nineteenth-century architecture. The
explanation, he thinks, is easy:

> Architecture got left behind in the march of Progress, and architects
> found themselves in a wholly artificial position, living and working
> in an unreal world. Having . . . lost touch and confidence, they were
> driven to look back instead of forward; and what we call their bad
> taste was simply 'taste' exercised far too independently of the real
> function of architecture.
> In the previous century, the eighteenth, everything was straight-
> forward.[53]

Apart from pursuing the chimera of the march of Progress and what
it does or does not force unwitting humans to do, Richards sets up
a false antithesis between the 'straightforward' eighteenth century
and the stylistically varied nineteenth century. In fact, stylistic
variety was one aspect of the eighteenth-century neo-Classical
movement and nothing to do with some supposed loss of 'touch
and confidence' by Victorian architects, still less with eighteenth-
century social structure as Richards seems to suppose:

> Now in the eighteenth century this quality of consistency was closely
> bound up with the social structure. The educated class was a small
> one numerically, but it was still the ruling class and took an active
> interest in architecture. There was therefore only one source of style,
> only one mould of fashion.[54]

He goes on very questionably to argue from this position that
Victorian architectural style was the consequence of the rise of a
class of coarse uneducated captains of industry. This argument is

used to establish a notion of modern architecture which is, by contrast, collective and anonymous. The idea of collective artistic achievement is a simple application of the idea of the *Zeitgeist* incarnated in the anonymous *Volk* – a theme familiar in the work of Herder and other Romantic populists. Richards claims that if anyone dares to criticize modern architects it will be because 'they forget that they are looking at people as individuals, whereas it is people as Society that architecture has to cater for'.[55] This collectivist and progressive view is emphatically underlined: 'It has been said before that great architecture is more a product of the times than of personalities.'[56] There must be no personality because there must be no memory: that is the essence of the doctrine of the *tabula rasa* which we achieve by 'avoiding a preconceived idea of what a building is going to look like (which is the basis of the Victorian view of architecture as large-scale sculpture), but, instead, taking absolutely nothing for granted'.[57] This Romantic Rousseauesque outlook leads Richards to accept at face value the 'cult of simplicity' of the English Arts and Crafts movement and of Voysey in particular. Voysey's large but coy pebble-dashed cottages with their artistically placed water-butts and shutters pierced with heart-shapes had already been appreciated by Pevsner, though not by Goodhart-Rendel who rightly identified their message as 'only-little-me-ishness'.[58] Richards followed Pevsner's line and was therefore able to believe that Voysey 'was one of the people who made modern architecture possible because he discarded "styles" and allowed the job to be done to be the source of style, instead of a historical precedent or accumulation of precedents selected by the architect'.[59] Norman Shaw's Bedford Park, a Picturesque suburb or make-believe village for the well-off middle class with artistic leanings, is also hailed by Richards as a great blow struck for ruthless modernity and unashamed truth, a step in time with 'the march of Progress' or, as he describes it, 'another breath of nature let into the artificiality of architectural fancy dress'.[60] In fact it had as much to do with the so-called realities of the contemporary situation as Marie Antoinette's *hameau* at Versailles, to which it was, in some ways, quite closely related.

60

While Richards, the *Architectural Review*, and even Summerson,[†] were preaching commitment to modern design as an essential instrument in the process of Building a Better Britain, an *émigré* Swiss in America was developing a yet more grandiose vision of modern architecture which appeared in book form in 1941 under the title, *Space, Time and Architecture: the Growth of a New Tradition*. The author, Sigfried Giedion, had been a pupil of Wölfflin at Munich, and in 1938 became a professor at Harvard University. *Space, Time and Architecture*, which he described as the product of 'stimulating association with young Americans',[61] was a publication of his Charles Eliot Norton lectures of 1938–9. From the start the book enjoyed wide popularity on both sides of the Atlantic and, through five editions and sixteen printings, it has grown to nearly one thousand pages and been translated into six languages. It is described on the dust-jacket of the current edition as 'a milestone in modern thought', while Walter Gropius has called it 'the standard work on the development of modern architecture'.

The portentous therapeutic role of the book as a bringer of 'wholeness' to modern society is stated in the opening words of the Foreword to the first edition:

> *Space, Time and Architecture* is intended for those who are alarmed by the present state of our culture and anxious to find a way out of the apparent chaos of its contradictory tendencies.
>
> I have attempted to establish, both by argument and by objective evidence, that in spite of the seeming confusion there is nevertheless a true, if hidden, unity, a secret synthesis, in our present civilization. To point out *why* this synthesis has *not* become *a conscious and active reality* has been one of my chief aims.[62]

The book is thus inspired by a belief that some universally accepted synthesis, some permanent modern consensus, is just around the

---

[†] In his Introduction to T. Dannatt's *Modern Architecture in Britain*, 1959, p. 19, Summerson wrote of the impact of the Labour election victory of 1945: 'Nevertheless 1945–51 was something much more than a vigorous convalescence. It altered irrevocably the national meaning of architecture.'

corner. This belief depends on what Popper called historicism: 'the view that the story of mankind has a plot, and that if we can succeed in unravelling this plot, we shall hold the key to the future.'[63] The 'secret synthesis' will not, of course, have any of the characteristics of 'style' since that would mark it out as something essentially transient. Thus Giedion writes:

> There is a word we should refrain from using to describe contemporary architecture – 'style'. The moment we fence architecture within a notion of 'style', we open the door to a formalistic approach. The contemporary movement is not a 'style' in the nineteenth-century meaning of form characterization. It is an approach to the life that slumbers unconsciously within all of us.[64]

Giedion hints at the idea of the collective unconscious in which all creative activity occurs. This was a characteristic of German romantics like Herder, Lazarus, and Steinthal, and is connected with the idea of genius as the conscious expression of the unconscious imagination of the folk-soul. The impact of Giedion's all-embracing totalitarian argument, with its aim of silencing all discussion, is to some extent softened by the pretentious language such as the belief in 'the life that slumbers unconsciously within all of us' or that in the work of twentieth-century architects 'past, present and future merge together as the indivisible wholeness of human destiny'.[65] Pretentious, too, is the implication of both title and text that the architectural synthesis he is proposing will have a specially unchallengeable position because of its harmony with the Space-Time conception of the universe defined in modern physics. He claims in the Foreword that his book shows 'the similarity of methods that are in use today in architecture, construction, painting, city planning and science',[66] though what this means in practice is frequent reference to the concept of Space-Time in architecture and one, only one, reference to Einstein. That this concept is of central importance to his message, is a vital part of our slumbering life and of the still unrealized but inevitably emergent 'indivisible wholeness' of our destiny, is made clear in the titles of the various parts of the book: for example, 'Space-Time in Art, Architecture and Construction', and 'Space-Time in City Planning'. On analysis, however, it turns out to be simply the nine-teenth-century German theories, as refined by Wölfflin, of spatial expression in art: 'the way volumes are placed in space and relate to one another, the way interior space is separated from exterior space or is perforated by it to bring about an interpenetration.'[67] Doubtless this spatial preoccupation still has a useful role as an art-historical tool,[68] but to hold it up as the solution of the ills of modern life is as inappropriate as Pugin's similar claims for Gothic architecture.

Giedion's interpretation of Space-Time becomes less exalted in tone, though no more sober in substance, as the book progresses. It turns out to be a feature of urban motorways, so that the caption to an illustration of the Randall Island clover-leaf intersection and Triborough Bridge in New York City describes the scene depicted as 'expressive of the space-time conception both in structure and handling of movement'.[69] Space-Time is being in a traffic jam: 'City-dwellers moving across congested avenues seem almost to know what is taking place behind them. This kind of spatio-temporal awareness was unknown in Baroque times; it may be a case of the re-development of a primitive sense.'[70]

Giedion's belief that he is going to reveal the 'secret synthesis' of the apparently conflicting tendencies of the modern world derives from the tradition of neo-Hegelian *Geistesgeschichte* in which he was brought up, and which tends to imply that men are of interest only in so far as they conform to the unarticulated spirit of their age which is struggling towards realization. This goes for the historian as well as those he studies:

The historian, the historian of architecture especially, must be in close contact with contemporary conceptions. Only when he is per-meated by the spirit of his own time is he prepared to detect those tracts of the past which previous generations have over-looked. . . . Indeed the historian in every field must be united with his own time by as widespread a system of roots as possible. . . . The historian must be intimately a part of his own period to know what questions concerning the past are significant to it. . . . The historian detached from the life of his own time writes irrelevant history, deals in frozen facts.[71]

Yet one can surely be suspicious of the implication that the historian owes less to documentary evidence than to inspiration by the spirit of his age. According to this view, as expressed in the writings of Karl Mannheim,[†] the historian is not capable of discovering truths by the scholarly exercise of a disciplined mind, but is merely a vehicle of the spirit of the age or of class interests or of the collective unconscious. Basic to this interpretation of history is a belief not merely in the spirit of the age but that the spirit expresses itself through men, rather than that men themselves create and constitute the spirit of the age and are able to help choose what it will be. It is a view which sees art and architecture as an inevitable reflection or expression of something else outside its creators. Giedion was quite clear about it when he wrote:

We are looking for the reflection in architecture of the progress our own period has made toward consciousness of itself . . . Everything in it [i.e. architecture], from its fondness for certain shapes to the approaches to specific building problems which it finds most natural, reflects the conditions of the age from which it springs. It is the product of all sorts of factors – social, economic, scientific, technical, ethnological.

However much a period may try to disguise itself, its real nature will still show through its architecture, whether this uses original forms of expression or attempts to copy bygone epochs. We recognise the character of the age as easily as we identify a friend's handwriting beneath attempted disguises. It is as an unmistakable index to

---

† See K. Mannheim, *Essays on the Sociology of Knowledge* (ed. P. Kecskemeti, 1972) and E. Shils, '*Ideology and Utopia* by Karl Mannheim', *Daedalus, Jnl. of the American Academy of Arts and Sciences*, Virginia, 1973, pp. 83–9.

what was really going on in a period that architecture is indispensable when we are seeking to evaluate that period.

In the great architectural masterpieces, as in every great work of art, the human shortcomings which every period exhibits so liberally fall away. This is why these works are true monuments of their epochs; with the overlay of recurrent human weaknesses removed, the central drives of the time of their creation show plainly.[72]

The basic Hegelian assumptions in such a passage derive immediately from Burckhardt who had, of course, taught Giedion's own master, Wölfflin. Burckhardt had expressed a belief that: 'Every cultural epoch which presents itself as a complete and articulate whole expresses itself not only in the life of the state, in religion, art and science, but also imparts its individual character to social life as such.'[73] He also, as Gombrich points out, gave this advice to a friend who wanted to write on Netherlandish art: 'Conceive your task as follows. How does the spirit of the fifteenth century express itself in painting? Then everything becomes simple.'[74] In challenging the validity of such an approach Gombrich remarks, 'It is one thing to see the interconnectedness of things, another to postulate that all aspects of a culture can be traced back to one key cause of which they are the manifestation.'[75] Gombrich goes on to argue that: 'it is this belief in the existence of an independent supra-individual collective spirit which seems to me to have blocked the emergence of a true cultural history. . . . I hope and believe cultural history will make progress if it also fixes attention firmly on the individual human being.'[76]

Giedion, however, believes in the importance of 'the central drives of the time' and, by contrast, in the relative insignificance of individuals who may even have been foolish enough to attempt, inevitably unsuccessfully, to resist them. For him each age has what he calls 'constituent facts'[†] and 'transitory facts'. The former are the great absolutes of the age which drive us forwards to endless

---

[†] This emphasis may have been derived from Viollet-le-Duc's belief in 'éléments constituifs'.

progress and have binding claims over us which we resist at our peril: 'Constituent facts are those tendencies which, when they are suppressed, inevitably reappear. Their recurrence makes us aware that these are elements which, all together, are producing a *new tradition.*' When Giedion goes on to tell us what some of these 'constituent facts' are, we come sharply down to earth and discover that they are no more than his own tastes and fancies: 'Constituent facts in architecture, for example, are the undulation of the wall, the juxtaposition of nature and the human dwelling, the open ground-plan.'[77] But who can pretend that a preference for an undulating rather than a straight wall represents some permanent and unchallengeable reality? Or, by the same token, that the man who sometimes wants a room he can be alone in, with a door he can shut, is asking for the impossible by ignoring the 'constituent fact' of 'the open ground-plan'? The whole process of reasoning is arbitrary. In disparaging existing traditions and arguing that new ones are necessary, critics such as Giedion base their arguments on allegedly existent but in fact arbitrarily constructed 'facts'.

Whereas constituent facts are 'recurrent and cumulative tendencies', transitory facts are merely 'sporadic trends'. Of these he writes, 'Facts of the other sort – equally the work of forces moving in a period – lack the stuff of permanence and fail to attach themselves to a new tradition.' Again, they turn out to be cultural developments of which Giedion happens to disapprove:

> Sometimes they are interlaced with every refinement of fashion – the furniture of the Second Empire in France is an instance. These we shall call transitory facts . . . The entire output of official painting was a transitory fact of that period [i.e. the nineteenth century], almost wholly without significance to the present day.[78]

Comparing and contrasting the value of constituent and transitory facts, he concludes: 'There is, however, no doubt which of these two classes of trends is the more likely to produce a solution of the real problems of the day.' Returning to the theme later in the book, he writes of what he calls 'official' art:

With no serious aims and no standards of its own, the most such an art could hope for was a financial success, and this it often achieved . . . The half dozen painters who carried on the artist's real work of invention and research were absolutely ignored. The constituent facts in the painting of our period were developed against the will of the public and almost in secret . . . The same situation held for architecture . . . The architect and the painter were faced with the same long struggle against *trompe l'oeil*. Both had to combat entrenched styles by returning to the pure means of expression. For some four decades painter after painter makes the effort to reconquer the plane surface. We have seen how the same struggle arose in architecture as a consequence of the demand for morality.[79]

Giedion evidently sees the role of art and architecture as a great moral struggle to 'produce a solution of the real problems of the day' by finding through scientific means – 'invention and research' – some permanent and 'pure means of expression' from which everything temporal, transitory, and even human, will have been eliminated. Giedion's vision is a parallel to the Marxist-Hegelian view of the end of history: that man will only become his true original self, will only re-assert himself in his original nature, when he is freed from the state of alienation brought about by the tyranny of private property. Giedion's holistic approach, inspired by Wölfflin's belief that: 'What matter are not the individual products of an age, but the fundamental temper which produced them',[80] serves to underline the suggestion we made earlier that Pugin's writings lent support to those who wished to establish a way of building that was not artificial, not marked by human imperfections, and which represented some inescapable but not yet fully appreciated or achieved reality. Not only is there a view that art and architecture are an inevitable reflection of something else: but it is clear that it is that other thing to which the critic is really committed. Whereas Pugin was at least honest with us about what that other thing was – a society dominated by the Catholic Church in the form she had taken in the Middle Ages – subsequent critics have often been far less clear. We are left to guess from hints in their writings that it is some utilitarian, egalitarian pattern of society inspired by the current progressive orthodoxies and alleged to be the true destiny of man.

In his booklet, *In Search of Cultural History*, Gombrich attacked the rather credulous determinism which we have seen as character-istic of the writers we have been discussing. He claimed that the cultural historian

> will not deny that the success of certain styles may be symptomatic of changing attitudes, but he will resist the temptation to use chang-ing styles and changing fashions as indicators of profound psycho-logical changes. The fact that we cannot assume such automatic connections makes it more interesting to find out if and when they may have existed.[81]

In challenging what he called 'the belief in the Hegelian wheel and in the need to survey the apparently God-given separate aspects of a culture from one privileged centre', Gombrich concluded that: 'This Hegelian wheel is really a secularized diagram of the Divine plan; the search for a centre that determines the total pattern of a civilization is consequently no more, but also no less, than the quest for an initiation into God's ways with man.'[82]

Giedion's book, *Mechanization Takes Command, a Contribution to Anonymous History*, 1948, extends the ideas developed in *Space, Time and Architecture*. The strange division of cultural achievement into 'constituent' and 'transitory' categories is, again, an important part of Giedion's technique. The urgency with which this doctrine is propagated derives from the identification of art with life itself and from the consequent belief that art must be 'real', must not be a style or a creative fantasy developing its own internal traditions. This view is clearly expressed in the following condemnation of nineteenth-century poetry and interior design: 'No less than the poetry of the ruling taste, intimate surroundings were created reflectively. Lacking was the leap into the unknown, the inventive. A powerful side of the nineteenth century is here revealed: the mask-like. Its view of real life is as deceptive as that of a wax museum.'[83] This passage also reminds us of the extent to which Giedion believes that the artist's capacity for reflecting on a tradition will have a stultifying rather than a creative impact on his work, will prevent rather than stimulate invention. Giedion's ideal is, once more, that old chimera: the *tabula rasa*. He writes of twentieth-century furniture design: 'As in painting and architecture, it was necessary temporarily to forget everything and begin afresh, as if no chair had ever before been built.'[84] This pursuit of novelty meant that in the 1920s 'for the first time since the eighteenth century, the room and its contents were felt as a single entity'. This absurd claim, which ignores the countless interior designers of the nineteenth century from Pugin to Guimard, is a consequence of the high valuation which Giedion places on 'novelty', which leads him to insist that modern design must always be doing something totally new even when it is evident that it is not.

The attack on tradition seems to be related to the view we identified earlier that art is life. This view also tends to narrow rather than broaden our possibilities of enjoyment, since it leads us to withdraw our sympathies from cultural phenomena produced in societies of which we may happen to disapprove on political, moral, or religious grounds. The Empire Style is a key example. Giedion disapproves of it both because he sees it as the expression of a man of whom he disapproves, Napoleon, and also because it re-uses symbolic forms in new contexts. We see here how the determinist and historicist belief that particular forms must be irretrievably rooted in a particular period and way of life rules out the possibility that the forms could acquire different meanings in different contexts. The important section of the book which develops this argument is called 'Napoleon and the Devaluation of Symbols'.† In it Giedion claims that 'what takes place in the Empire style is nothing other than a devaluation of symbols. As Napoleon devaluated nobility, so he devaluated ornament.'[85] Furthermore, the Empire Style was socially unacceptable because it somehow conflicted with the demands of 'reality', that is to say it did not conform to Giedion's notions of what life ought to have been like at the time:

---

† It was given special prominence by being printed as an article in the *Architectural Review* in November 1947 shortly before the publication of the book itself.

'Percier and Fontaine, and the Empire style they created in all its ramifications, yield the key to an understanding of the nineteenth century. They are the first representatives of the ruling taste, which pushed isolated forms into prominence and shrank from the under-lying reality of a thing.'[86] Giedion praises William Morris for react-ing against this tradition, yet hails him not as a designer of superlative brilliance and imagination developing from medieval and early Renaissance traditions, but as someone who made a moral stand against the lack of 'reality' which is supposed to characterize earlier nineteenth-century design: 'The circle around William Morris strives for morally pure forms.'[87] Yet those who chose to imitate Morris failed to sustain his high reforming tone, and thus 'the moral purity of Morris's teaching was lost as it became recon-ciled to the ruling taste'.[88]

Another aspect of the 'ruling taste' which particularly worries Giedion is what he calls 'cushion furniture'. He finds untruthful-ness and unreality expressed, for example, in the way in which it conceals its structure, and he interprets this as evidence of deep inner unrest. However, he feels that modern art has now supplied us with the 'key' to such problems: 'The Surrealists have given us keys to the psychic unrest that haunted mechanized ornament, cushion furniture, and the whole interior.'[89]

3. Furneaux Jordan

If Giedion stands as a key example of the interpretation of archi-tecture through the *Zeitgeist*, Robert Furneaux Jordan is a striking example of the vulgar sociological interpretation. Jordan's *Victorian Architecture* (1966) is not a book for people interested in the achieve-ments of Victorian architects, but rather a potted analysis of archi-tectural history in terms of the dominance and succession of ruling classes.[†] Like Pevsner's *Pioneers of the Modern Movement*, it is funda-

---

[†] The book is in a line of development from F.D. Klingender's *Art and the Industrial Revolution*, 1947.

mentally a plea for the Modern Movement and ends up, surpriz-
ingly, with photographs of Pevsner's favourite modern German
buildings by Behrens and Gropius. In fact the book is only ostensibly about Victorian architecture: he does not analyse or describe
any buildings in detail and, an astonishing lacuna, there is not a
single plan in the whole book and certainly nothing so advanced as
a cross-section. It is in a way unfair to serious scholars like Viollet-
le-Duc or Pevsner to include in a book which discusses their work
an account of a popular journalist like Jordan. However, we should
spend a moment with his *Victorian Architecture*, first, because of its
undoubted influence on students and on the general public as the
only book available on its subject, and secondly, because it is a low
vulgarization of ideas which had been originally propounded by
Pevsner himself.[†]

The prerequisite for such a history of nineteenth- and early
twentieth-century art is to divide it up so that it reflects an incessant
class struggle between the 'haves' and the 'have-nots'. It is a false and
even inhuman view, since in ignoring the individual it ignores the
delicate and infinitely subtle nuances and gradations of English
society which have formed the subject of so much English literature
from at least the eighteenth century to the present day. Nevertheless,
Jordan pursues relentlessly his simple idea that there must be an
artistic parallel to the struggle of workers against masters. Thus
romanticism is seen as a revolt against the aristocracy: 'In the
nineteenth century the romantic . . . was still, as always, a rebel against
aristocracy and academic traditions',[90] while the anecdotal sentiment
of Victorian painting 'helped to lay the foundations of the Welfare

---

[†] An example of the determinist and materialist view that visual form is always a
predictable expression of something else is Pevsner's belief that the Italian
Renaissance Revival of Barry's London club-houses can be accounted for 'because
it reminded their members of an age of prosperous cultured merchants' (*An Outline
of European Architecture* (1943), 1945 edn., p. 209). Yet if we turn to the documentary sources to discover who were the men on the Travellers' Club committee who
actually commissioned what was the first and most influential of the Italianate
club-houses, we find no merchants nor any reason to suppose that the members
wished to be associated with a mercantile way of life.

State a hundred years later'.[91] Romanticism is also 'the beat culture of its day'.[92] In fact, romanticism is anything of which Jordan happens to approve: for example, each of the names in the following list was 'opposed in some way or other to what we would call "the Establishment"': they are 'Turner, Constable, Girtin, Walter Scott, Samuel Palmer, Blake, Shelley, Keats, Coleridge, Wordsworth, Byron, Charlotte Yonge, Pugin, Butterfield, Gilbert Scott, Pater, Christina Rossetti, the six pre-Raphaelites, Ruskin, Morris, Newman, Keble, Carlyle, Emily Brontë, the Brownings and Tennyson'.[93] Certainly all these expressed dissatisfaction with the state of the world: in the case of the Christians in the list this is scarcely surprising, since the doctrine of the Fall causes every Christian to believe that the world is imperfect. It is erroneous, however, to assume that anyone who expresses this dissatisfaction for whatever reason becomes necessarily an ally of socialism. The list is, moreover, valueless because it attempts to unite such richly diverse talents on the grounds of their alleged opposition to a never-defined Establishment; it is particularly misleading when it includes men like Walter Scott, Wordsworth, Coleridge, Newman, and Tennyson, all of whom eventually preached differing versions of a kind of High Toryism.

The loose language and slipshod scholarship, which everywhere goes with vulgar Marxism and with its dichotomy of society into 'workers' and 'masters', is typified in the following passage, by no means extreme compared with others in the book, but sufficiently condensed and self-contained to make a suitable quotation:

> With the shift from an agricultural to an industrial England, an old and well-defined society vanished. On the one hand there had been the gentry—nobility, squirearchy and professions; on the other there had been the peasantry. (Symbolically the Reform Act of 1832 marks the passing of the former, the Education Act of 1870 the passing of the latter.) The gentry had for too long been the patrons of a 'polite' and elegant classicism – the very insignia of their status being the Adam fireplace or Georgian doorway; while the peasantry had been the patrons of the pedlar, of the ancient crafts and those immemorial ways of building that we call the vernacular.[94]

In fact the Industrial Revolution by no means killed off the old aristocratic society, since many of the nobility grew rich from its proceeds. The old society in England was never 'well defined' because, unlike continental society, it allowed for movement up and down the social scale and consequent ambiguity of social status. If one had to range classes against each other, instead of setting gentry against peasantry one might with equal (i.e. with very little) justice choose to set the nobility and the peasantry together against the commercial and professional classes who were the 'newcomers'. It is also absurd to suggest that Georgian design was a socially divisive force, since there can have been few styles so lacking in political overtones and few which have become such a norm throughout a social hierarchy, so that basically the only difference between the sash-windows inserted into St. James's Palace and into the village inn was one of size. Furthermore, it is doubtful how far the peasantry were in a position to give patronage to any form of building. Rural vernacular buildings on the country estates depended on farmers and landowners, industrial vernacular on professional men and industrialists, so the idea that there is some deep class hostility between Georgian and vernacular is pure fantasy.

This fantasy is rooted in the author's populistic chauvinism which believes that there is some permanent essentially English way of building which has been forced beneath the surface as a result of the importation of foreign tastes and which can only be recovered after the socialist revolution. It is a view which echoes Cobbett's belief that the peasantry were the true Englishmen while the higher classes were foreigners, i.e. Normans. Thus in Jordan's view the buildings of England from the early seventeenth to the early nineteenth centuries – from Inigo Jones to John Soane – 'do after all represent only an imported art. They are part only of an aristocratic culture, not part of the long vernacular, universal, native or national art of the English people'.[95] But what can it mean to say, for example, that Wren's City churches, which were the pride of the prosperous commercial parishes of the seventeenth-century City of London, or that the red-brick houses of hop-growers and doctors in Georgian Farnham, or that Adam's Edinburgh University, or Soane's Dulwich

Gallery, are all aristocratic and not native? What can it mean, more-over, to argue that Pugin's and Barry's New Palace of Westminster, as compared with Nash's Carlton House Terrace, 'symbolizes the change from an aristocratic to a democratic art'?[96] It can mean nothing at all, since Barry's masterpiece is in a far more luxurious and alien style than any Georgian public building. Jordan's hatred of those whom he chooses to regard as aristocrats certainly does not help him to make discriminating judgements: thus he observes of Ashridge Park and Culzean, Eastnor, Belvoir, Killy Moon, and East Cowes castles that they are houses which 'became outmoded ulti-mately, less because of changes in fashion, taste or style, less because of their inherent unreality and absurdity, than because the sort of people for whom they were built were fortunately eliminated from society'.[97] The first four houses were built for peers, so they inevi-tably offend Jordan, but Killy Moon was built for Colonel William Stewart, M.P., and East Cowes by the architect Nash for his own occupation. Soldiers, politicians, and architects have scarcely been eliminated from society, even in Communist countries. What, too, does Jordan mean by 'outmoded'? In the sense that styles always change, then the houses are necessarily outmoded, but he specifi-cally excludes that interpretation. Nor is it easy to interpret his censure in terms of function, since Eastnor, Belvoir, and Killy Moon are all privately inhabited houses, Culzean is successfully run by the National Trust for Scotland and is also used for entertaining state vis-itors, Ashridge is the college it always looked like even when it was a private house, while, ironically, the only one that has been demo-lished is East Cowes, the 'purpose-built' architect's house. Jordan's view implies that a work of art loses its value if its original patron is dead or if his descendants no longer wield political power.

Another passage from *Victorian Architecture* will show the intellec-tual and moral muddle consequent upon the belief that the unreal-ized potentialities of the emergent *Zeitgeist* or of society provide a basis for the assessment of works of art:

But if we take everything into account – the social as well as the architectural implications of the Red House – its significance *was* profound. Until then the architecture of the great Victorian houses had consisted mainly of the imposition of new stylistic variations upon basically eighteenth-century themes. With the Red House, with Philip Webb, with the emergence of the young Norman Shaw and with Morrisian ideals of craftsmanship hovering, as it were, in the wings, the change is obvious. Far off we can sniff the twentieth century upon the wind.

For one thing the change was social. It was a change of patronage. If men like Barry had troubled themselves to establish the social status of the architect that was no more than recognition by them that the eighteenth-century class structure was trying to perpetuate itself into a century where, clearly, it was destined to die. Barry and his like loved a lord, and built for lords. But the cool, rational eighteenth-century mind – concerned with 'taste' but indifferent to what others thought – was no longer enough. Barry, through architecture, had to make, for his patrons, the last great gesture. These London palaces of the Victorian hostesses, these country mansions of the big house parties, were *meant* to express social grandeur. And this last self-assertion of a dying aristocracy was necessarily vulgar. The aristocratic principle could no longer be taken for granted; it had to draw attention to itself.[98]

First of all the Red House. It is quite untrue to suggest that planning remained essentially Georgian or symmetrical till 1859. The free plan was the creation of the eighteenth-century Picturesque movement, as developed in the work of Nash and carried into the early Victorian period by an architect like Salvin – neither of whom, incidentally, would have been guilty of the glum planning of the Red House where all the principal rooms face north. The Red House did not establish 'a change of patronage'. Had no commoner ever commissioned a house before? What, for example, was Thomas Hope doing when, supported like Morris by a commercial fortune, he commissioned his Duchess Street and Deepdene houses and designed special furniture and fittings for them because, so he claimed, he could find none of sufficient craftsmanship and quality in the shops?[99] Yet no one has claimed that we can 'sniff the twentieth century' at Duchess Street.

It is also untrue, of course, to suggest that elaborate country houses were designed only for the 'dying aristocracy'. They appealed to a tremendous variety of clients: nobility, gentry, *nouveaux riches*, artists, architects, politicians, and one simply cannot tell by looking at them which were built for whom, though some will probably look vulgar to us and others will not.[†]

Jordan believes that 'in the nineteenth century something happened to the human mind – a change of an almost biological order, a change in Man's attitude to the whole world outside himself'.[100] In the dawn of this age the Gothic Revival, indeed any revival, was particularly reprehensible; thus he writes: 'An artificially revived architecture was the natural corollary of an artificially revived religion.'[101]

There is no pleasing Mr. Jordan. Take C.R. Cockerell, who designed few churches or country houses, those building types of which Jordan so frequently disapproves: though more at home in aristocratic circles than many of his fellow architects, Cockerell did not give himself up to country-house practice but chose rather to bring dignity and quality to the premises of banks and commercial companies and, indeed, established the image of a bank that has survived in most people's minds until the present time. Perhaps it is just that Jordan disapproves of banks, but for him Cockerell 'was clearly as far removed as could be from the realities of the century in which he lived . . . Cockerell's contribution to the life of his time, his influence upon that life, and upon our life is precisely nil'.[102] What, then, is the nature of this influence that Jordan believes that architects must exert? How is it to be measured? Did Michelangelo exert it, or Robert Adam, or Mies van der Rohe? What, in fact, are the kinds of things that we *can* say about architecture? In answering that question we are helped by Jordan's book which shows us clearly many of the kinds of things that we cannot reasonably say. We have

---

[†] Mark Girouard's *The Victorian Country House* (Oxford, 1971), shows how architectural history can be brilliantly effective as social or cultural history when attention is concentrated on what individuals did and not on notions of what classes must have done.

only spent this long with his book because it represents so completely the prejudices of the collectivist, anti-artistic, ideological viewpoint.

In 1966 Pevsner wrote in the Annual Report of the Victorian Society:

> I want to use my Chairman's page to praise a new book which you should all possess. Robert Furneaux Jordan with his Pelican *Victorian Architecture* has at last provided the right introduction to a subject which is so close to our hearts. The book is written with passion and beautifully illustrated throughout . . . and as far as sheer quality of writing is concerned the two introductory chapters, concentrating on social history, could not be bettered.[103]

Professor Pevsner is a great scholar. Furneaux Jordan is no scholar at all. It is interesting and enlightening, therefore, to examine Pevsner's own writings in order to understand how he could speak with such high praise about this wrong-headed book. In doing so we will fit the last stone into the bridge which spans the century between Pugin and Pevsner.

Only by throwing into relief the individual oneness of any given period or style or nation, and the logical coherence of all its utterances in the most varied fields of human activity, will the historiographer in the end be able to make his reader discover what form a certain problem must take at the present moment.

N. Pevsner, *Academies of Art Past and Present*,
Cambridge, 1940, p. ix.

The biographer can easily see a personal significance in these three hypothetical nationalities. But is there in the world a biographer who could lay his hand upon his heart and say that he would not have seen as much significance in any three other nationalities? If Browning's ancestors had been Frenchmen, should we not have said that it was from them doubtless that he inherited that logical ability which marks him among English poets? If his grandfather had been a Swede, should we not have said that the old sea-roving blood broke out in bold speculation and insatiable travel? If his great aunt had been a Red Indian should we not have said that only in the Ojibways and the Blackfeet do we find the Browning fantasticality combined with the Browning stoicism?

G.K. Chesterton, *Robert Browning*, 1903, pp. 6–7.

PART III

Pevsner

1. Early Writings

The scholarship of Sir Nikolaus Pevsner is so rich and capacious, his work so varied, extensive, and inclusive of so many of the different approaches we have been outlining, that analysis of his achievement illuminates a whole field of modern architectural history. Born in Leipzig in 1902, he was educated at the universities of Leipzig, Munich, Berlin, and Frankfurt. He specialized early in art history[†] and had prepared a doctoral dissertation on German Baroque architecture by 1924. He was influenced by two contrasting accounts of Italian sixteenth- and seventeenth-century art: Werner Weisbach's *Der Barock als Kunst der Gegenreformation* of 1921, and Wilhelm Pinder's lectures on Mannerism which he attended in 1922–4. His first major scholarly article, called 'Gegenreformation und Manierismus', appeared in 1925 in the *Repertorium für Kunstwissenschaft*. This important paper not only defined the painting of Mannerism for the first time, but also established the position which Pevsner has maintained ever since as one of the most significant continuators of the line descending from Burckhardt and Wölfflin. From the former he inherits his insistence on art history as an aspect of cultural and social history, from the latter a belief that in terms of art-historical method the spirit or style of the age is more important than the individual and

---

[†] He gives an interesting brief account of the influences on his early art-historical development in The American Association of Architectural Bibliographers, *Papers*, vii (ed. W.B. O'Neil), Virginia U.P., Charlottesville, 1970, pp. [vii]–xi.

varying achievements of great artists. Thus in summing up the
theme of the paper in 1968, Pevsner emphasized 'that Pontormo,
Federigo Zuccari, Barocci and Tintoretto all have essential features
in common and that they are features expressing the spiritual state
of Italy during the same period'.[1] What Pevsner means by 'the spiritual state of Italy' is made clear enough in his summary of some
Counter-Reformation personalities and ideas, which was drawn
from Pastor's *The History of the Popes* and coloured by a conventional North European or Protestant idea of 'Jesuitry'. Thus
Pevsner's chilling picture of the Jesuits where 'every motion of
individual will must be forcibly repressed' and where 'the attitude
of every subordinate is one of total passivity',[2] merely echoes
Wölfflin's idea that 'the Jesuits forced their spiritual system on the
individual and made him sacrifice his rights to the idea of the
whole'.[3] Pevsner establishes a pattern somewhat carelessly in the
religious sphere, and then transposes it arbitrarily to a description
of a style of painting.

With his own picture of 'the spiritual state of Italy' before him,
Pevsner decides that there must be precise analogies to it in paint-
ing though he never explains why there should be. In
'Gegenreformation und Manierismus' he simply states:

Here again the parallel with the arts is obvious. Dvořák showed that
the suppression of the individual significance of the human being lies
at the heart of the last phase of Michelangelo's work. The mature art
of Tintoretto (born 1528) and Barocci (born 1526) subordinates the
human figure to an abstract linear schema; and in the work of Vasari
(born 1511), Salviati (born 1510), Zuccaro (born 1529) and his
school, the Bolognese and the Milanese, the individual form loses its
significance in favour of unmanageably crowded or decoratively-
ordered pictorial elements. This negation of the individual significance of the human being, this constraint which submerges it in a
welter of forms, stretches it out of its natural shape, or immobilizes
it in heavy draperies, constitutes the deepest and most important link
between the art of Mannerism and the dominant ideas of the age of
the Counter-Reformation.[4]

That Mannerist art suppresses the individual significance of the human being is, however unlikely, a point that could be debated; but surely the whole tradition of Christian spirituality is of its very nature opposed to any such suppression. Moreover, do artists like Bronzino and El Greco really immobilize the human being in heavy draperies, and even if they do can it really make sense to see it as a reflection of the spirit which produced the *Spiritual Exercises* of St. Ignatius Loyola? After all, artistic creation has its own internal traditions and is not simply a reflex of events outside the artistic sphere. But there is yet more for which the Jesuits are held responsible: Pevsner refers to 'the Jesuit attitude to human weakness and sin' as one where 'Tolerance was the rule, especially where powerful people were concerned. Rather forgive too much than give a soul up for lost. Only in cases of genuine heresy, i.e. wilful obstinacy, was rigour considered essential. Here too is the germ of a Baroque characteristic: moral relativism.'[5] The language again suggests a lack of familiarity with the customs and doctrines of the Church he is writing about: in this case the sacrament of penance which alone is the context within which the priest has the power to forgive sins and then only if the penitent purposes amendment for the future. Exactly what is meant by the 'moral relativism' of the Baroque, or how it could be discerned in a style of painting, is not made clear. Instead, in a passage which shows how free Pevsner can sometimes be in the construction of parallels between the various spheres of life, he passes on to the character of St Pius V. This pope is supposed to represent the quintessence of all this Jesuitry since his 'life was a model of asceticism. . . . At midday, he would take bread soup, two eggs and half a glass of wine; in the evening vegetable soup, salad, shellfish and boiled fruit.' This quite nourishing and substantial fare is described as an

astonishing state of affairs [which] was not the product of the austerity of one individual. The whole city seems to have experienced a crisis of introspection. This is proved not only by Michelangelo's last style as a sculptor, exactly contemporary with the pontificate of Pius V, or by the fact that he offered to build the Jesuit church in Rome free of charge, but the failure of the Roman people as a whole to react in any way against the prevailing austerity.[6]

Pevsner's argument here is absolutely explicit: knowing Michelangelo's late style as a sculptor enables us to 'prove' that it 'must' have been accompanied by 'a crisis of introspection' throughout the city of Rome; and we have already deduced this crisis from knowledge of the Pope's eating habits. Such schematic analysis, guided by a theory rather than by documentary evidence, is characteristic of the great tradition of Hegelian *Geistesgeschichte* but is particularly unconvincing when applied to an artist of the gigantic stature and individuality of Michelangelo, whose stylistic development was probably more inward than that of any other great European artist. Indeed, he was strongly opposed politically to his Medici patrons in Florence.

Something else for which Jesuitry is held responsible is eroticism, because 'only an age preoccupied with metaphysical objectives could have witnessed the introduction of lasciviousness into the major arts'. Yet surely medieval spirituality was no less metaphysical? In fact, having argued that eroticism is a necessary consequence of the spirit of the age, Pevsner points out 'the total absence of eroticism in the most important Mannerists, Tintoretto, Bassano, El Greco, Barocci, Cerano, Zuccaro and Calvaert'.[7] Here, then, Pevsner's belief in the *Zeitgeist* has led him to support Wölfflin's view that 'What matter are not the individual products of an age but the fundamental temper which produced them',[8] since what Pevsner is saying is that the 'fundamental temper' of the age must have been erotic even if the 'individual products' happened not to be.

Many of the arguments and historical or religious analogies brought forward in this article were repeated in an important essay on 'The Architecture of Mannerism' published more than two decades later. The different styles of Sanmicheli, Giulio Romano, Peruzzi, Michelangelo, Vasari, and Ammanati were all explained away as a consequence of the familiar Jesuit 'rigorous enforcement of no longer self-understood dogma'. 'What individualism had been developed by the Renaissance', Pevsner argued, 'was to be crushed, and yet could not be crushed.'[9] The essay contains many sensitive and illuminating accounts of individual buildings, and for that reason has been read with pleasure and profit by several generations of students; but it was undoubtedly generated by the belief that the forms of the buildings were merely emanations of the spirit of the age, and that the historian's role was to discern and disclose that inarticulate spirit working below the surface of particular events. Pevsner complained on the first page that Englishmen had never done this, that they had never been prepared to summon up what he called 'the final essence distilled out of all the individual qualities of all the leading personalities of one particular age'. He argued that, for example, 'Hobbes's and Spinoza's philosophy, Bernini's and Rembrandt's art, Richelieu's and Cromwell's statecraft have certain fundamentals in common, and on these we can establish a Baroque style of exact meaning. England has been characteristically slow in accepting this working hypothesis.'[10] There is inevitably a certain amount of arbitrariness in the distillation of an essence common to Bernini and Cromwell, Hobbes and Rembrandt. What is important for our purposes is the clear assumption that there is a 'spirit' or 'essence' which pervades and dominates all intellectual, artistic, and social activity. Artists are not individuals with unique imaginations and talents, but are only manifestations of this all-pervasive spirit or essence.

Having established in 1925 the existence of Mannerism as the style of the Italian sixteenth century, Pevsner went on to publish in the same journal three years later a paper called 'Beiträge zur Stilgeschichte des Früh- und Hoch-Barock' in order to clarify his ideas on the seventeenth century. It is an interesting and unusual study which, although ostensibly concerned with '*Stilgeschichte*', concentrates on broad theories about religion, science, and politics with very little emphasis on works of art. The theories were derived in general from Pastor, Ranke, Döllinger, and Weber, and to them Pevsner brings a view of religion familiar in the Protestant north – the countries of the Gothic cathedrals, the Reformation, and the

Gothic Revival. This is a view which, though not often explicitly expressed, believes in its heart of hearts that real Christianity was essentially medieval. This belief could have been acquired, ironically, from Christian architects like Pugin and Street who were bent on recovering the lost essence of Christian design which they believed had existed in the Middle Ages. The view was echoed by Emile Mâle in the closing words of his *L'Art religieux de la fin du moyen âge en France* (1908): 'Henceforth there would be no Christian Art, only Christian artists';[11] and has reappeared in new guise in the church today where it is fashionable to assume that the liturgical arrangements of the Early Christians represent some kind of permanent ideality undefiled by artificial accretions. Mâle, however, changed his views as a result of reading Weisbach's *Der Barock als Kunst der Gegenreformation.* Thus eleven years later he produced his own important study of *L'Art religieux après le Concile de Trente.* Pevsner, however, has never changed his views on this subject. In 'Beiträge zur Stilgeschichte des Früh-und Hoch-barock'[12] he is able to write of the seventeenth century: 'With the true realization of the infinity of the universe the idea of direct dependence on a personal God inevitably receded from the human consciousness.' In *An Outline of European Architecture* (1943) he was to take the even more Puginian line of dating the collapse of Christianity to the early fifteenth century. Describing church plans by Michelozzo and Brunelleschi he wrote:

> For a central plan is not an other-worldly, but a this-worldly conception. The prime function of the mediaeval church had been to lead the faithful to the altar. In a completely centralized building no such movement is possible. The building has its full effect only when it is looked at from the focal point. There the spectator must stand and, by standing there, he becomes himself 'the measure of all things'. Thus the religious meaning of the church is replaced by a human one.[13]

Once again, a sketchy picture of medieval religion is used as a basis for predicting the type of architecture which must have expressed it within the all-pervasive essence of the age. Thus the questionable belief that 'the prime function of the mediaeval church was to lead the faithful to the altar'[†] leads him to assume that a centralized church without a long nave leading to the altar must somehow be non-Christian. The same essentially Puginian view that the Renaissance struck a blow at the Christian faith is stated categorically in *The Leaves of Southwell* (1945). Describing the beauty of the naturalistically carved capitals of the late thirteenth-century Chapter House at Southwell Minster, Pevsner claims that 'The Renaissance in the South two hundred years later was perhaps once again capable of such worship of beauty, but no firm faith was left to strengthen it.'[14]

Again, in the descriptive notes he contributed to Sacheverell Sitwell's *German Baroque Sculpture* (1938), he allows unsupported assumptions about religion to account for artistic forms. He claims that 'the Protestant is led to direct and unaided intercourse with God; Catholic religious experience is chiefly communal',[15] and that this leads to a 'fundamentally different approach of Protestantism and Catholicism to the visual arts'. This false contrast ignores the influence on Protestants of Franciscan spirituality, of St. Bernard, and, in particular, of Thomas à Kempis's *The Imitation of Christ*, all of which formed the basis of nineteenth-century Protestant spirituality. Pevsner did not, of course, invent this view but merely inherited it from the nineteenth century which had actually produced doctored 'Protestant' editions of à Kempis, still being printed today, which omitted his fourth and concluding chapter, 'About the Blessed Sacrament'. The fallacious antithesis between Protestant and Catholic religious experience is used in the same paragraph, in a way with which we have now become familiar, to construct a *Zeitgeist* which will account for German Baroque sculpture: 'Therefore the apogee of Protestant art is music, of Catholic art sculpture, painting and decoration.' This view was not developed in

---

[†] Frequent communion for the laity was not a medieval custom and altars were generally shut off from them by screens. The objects to which the faithful were more likely to be led directly were shrines and reliquaries.

German Baroque Sculpture but assumed unexpected prominence five years later in *An Outline of European Architecture*. Chapter Six concludes with a resounding panegyric on Protestantism. The modern world, he argued, 'is that of Protestantism'. 'The Protestant countries . . . created . . . the Industrial Revolution in the material and the symphony in the spiritual world. What the cathedral had been to the Middle Ages, the symphony was to the nineteenth century.'[16] Now it is no part of the argument of the present book that Protestants can or cannot write symphonies or design buildings, but the statement that the Protestant countries produced the symphony must be challenged by simple facts. Of the principal composers of symphonies in the eighteenth and nineteenth centuries – Haydn, Mozart, Beethoven, Schubert, Berlioz, Mendelssohn, Schumann, Liszt, Brahms, Tchaikovsky, Dvořák, Bruckner, and Mahler – all were Catholics save for Beethoven, Schumann, Mendelssohn, Brahms, and Tchaikovsky. Beethoven and Tchaikovsky were scarcely Protestants whatever else they may have been – Beethoven might be described as a lapsed-Catholic deist – while Mahler was a Catholic convert, and Liszt received the four minor orders of the Catholic church.

Our description of Pevsner's methods in the formative years from 1925 has suggested his essentially determinist approach to art and architecture. Given a few selected abstractions about the nature of society and religion in a particular period, he will postulate the kind of art and architecture it must have produced. In *German Baroque Sculpture* he wrote of the German cultural revival of 1650–1750 that followed the Thirty Years War: 'The causes are manifold. Some economic and political reasons will be hinted at later, but the root of the revival must be found in a harmony between the style demanded by the century, and the inborn aesthetic, expressional qualities of the German.'[17]

We have hinted before that nationality has occasionally been claimed as the decisive determinant of artistic style. The imperatives of race or nation, familiar in modern German thought, were made the subject of a whole book, *The Englishness of English Art* (1955). The theme of this book had been occupying Pevsner since before

86

his arrival in this country in the 1930s. He began to deliver lectures on the subject in 1941 at Birkbeck College in the University of London, and chose to expand the theme when, after the war, he was invited by the B.B.C. to give the Reith Lectures. It was the text of these lectures which, doubled in size and attractively illustrated, he published in 1955.

In *The Englishness of English Art* Pevsner analyses what he considers to be the principal stylistic characteristics of English painting, sculpture, and architecture from the eleventh century to the present day, and attempts to account for them in terms of 'national character'. But in order to sustain the argument that there must be some unconscious synthesis, some underlying uniformity which will be a reflection of national character, the historian has to bring to his subject all sorts of assumptions about the national character, language, religion, politics, and so on. And these assumptions, unlike the art-historical assumptions, are rarely analysed or defended. Thus Pevsner brings forward a fair amount of evidence to support his notion that 'excessive length' is a feature of English architecture as in, for example, the perhaps rather strained comparison between the late Elizabethan Combination Room at St. John's College, Cambridge, and a Georgian terrace in Kensington. But the equally important non-visual characteristics of Englishness tend to be taken for granted and are supported by little evidence. Thus he mentions more than once that the national character is reflected in a language that is blunt and direct, and produces as evidence the contrast between the Italian word 'costoletta' and its English counterpart 'chop'. There is every reason, however, for choosing the more accurate and elegant little word 'cutlet' as the counterpart of 'costoletta'. However, our fundamental concern is not with these minor queries but with the impression left by the emphasis on national character or *Volksgeist* as a determinant of artistic style without due regard to artistic tradition and the imaginative and intellectual powers of the individual artist.

Pevsner does adhere unqualifiedly to the method which is characteristic of him, but there are times when he acknowledges that it is inadequate:

Sir John Soane's style is too personal, too idiosyncratic, to fit any system of period or national classification completely. It is the same as with Hawksmoor in the early eighteenth and Butterfield in the mid-nineteenth century. These men were laws unto themselves – as indeed on an infinitely vaster scale was Shakespeare – and they can only tenuously be tied to the categories of national character.[18]

An interpretation of English culture which has to leave out our greatest poet and three of our most significant architects is a very strange one, but presumably in line with that ambition defined at the beginning of the book of finding out 'what all works of art and architecture of one people have in common, at whatever time they may have been made'.[19]

The postulate of a kind of collective unconscious *Kunstwollen* lies behind Pevsner's little book *The Leaves of Southwell*, where he asserts a connection between the mid-thirteenth-century writings of the German Albertus Magnus, *De Animalibus* and *De Vegetabilibus*, and the late thirteenth-century carved capitals of the Chapter House at Southwell. But after ten pages of discussion and quotation he returns to the spirit of the age as the explanation and norm of artistic creation:

> So we are left with the only explanation which historical experience justifies; the existence of a spirit of the age, operating in art as well as philosophy, in religion as well as politics. This spirit works changes in style and outlook, and the man of genius is not he who tries to shake off its bonds, but he to whom it is given to express it in the most powerful form.[20]†

The denial of the role of the individual as a creative or significant force, and the belief that his role is that of a mere voice

---

† This same view is explicitly stated in the following passage: 'The illuminated manuscripts of the Reichenau, the sculptures of Reims, Giotto's frescoes were not created because of the existence of a live workshop tradition, but because of a Zeitgeist expressing itself in religion, politics and philosophy, in guild and in workshop.' (N. Pevsner, *Academies of Art Past and Present*, Cambridge, 1940, p. 224.)

through which the great unconscious consensus of the age can be expressed, are ideas familiar in nineteenth- and twentieth-century political philosophy. Many of the leading philosophers of the nineteenth century were conscious of living in an age in which traditional institutions, religion, and *mores* were crumbling. They sought to fill the gap with some broad, moral, utilitarian consensus which would govern all aspects of social, political, artistic, and educational endeavour. Men as varied as Mill, Arnold, Comte, and Marx all sought to find a firm basis of belief which could replace their uncertain religious faith. They called it by different names, nationalism, democracy, socialism, and so on, and they used language of moral doctrinal absoluteness from which the individual is allowed to have no appeal. We have already seen Pugin's relation to this tradition. In turning to Pevsner it is clear that when his art-historical method, in which a pervasive *Weltanschauung* took precedence over the actual works of art, was applied to the twentieth-century art he would contribute to and draw on the tradition which seeks to establish a collectivist religion of humanity.

2. *The Historic Mission*

In his early work Pevsner made interpretations of the intentions of artists and of the meanings of works of art which were calculated to fit into the pattern of a *Zeitgeist* which, in turn, he constructed from sometimes selective and partial studies of religion, philosophy, and history. We shall see in the present section of this book how, when he became a spokesman for the Modern Movement, he changed his ideas somewhat but not the fundamental theme of this thought. Whereas before he had been an analyst, now he became a protagonist of a certain type of art and architecture. In his first phase, when he was dealing with the past, he could not try to make the dead paint differently, but when he came to deal with the recent past and the present he became an agent of 'reform'. He tried to further one kind of art at the expense of another. But the principle of interpretation remained 'holistic', and the argument was still that art must be integral to society. Now, however, it went further and asserted that art must express the essence of a still unborn society struggling to realize the potentiality of a socialistic industrial technology overlain by the dying remains of Victorian capitalism. The new architecture was to be integral, not to contemporary society with its untidy individualism, but rather to the 'idea' of a socialist industrialism that had yet to be realized. The underlying principle remains the same throughout Pevsner's work: art must 'fit' into the *Zeitgeist* which is now a progressivist harbinger of the earthly new Jerusalem. This new art will be distinguished by truth, honesty, health, anonymity, and faith in technology and in the spirit of youth. This second phase of Pevsner's development is to be seen in certain major works: *Pioneers of the Modern Movement from William Morris to Walter Gropius* (1936), *An Enquiry into Industrial Art in England* (1937), and, to a lesser extent, *An Outline of European Architecture* (1943).

Pioneers of the Modern Movement assumed that a moral consensus of sociological and architectural import had been achieved by 1914 as an inevitable synthesis of conflicting nineteenth-century tendencies, and that it was not open to anyone to question or to remove himself from this consensus. To Pevsner the architecture he had in mind was the only one 'which fitted all those aspects which mattered, aspects of economics and sociology, of materials and function. It seemed folly to think that anyone would wish to abandon it.'[21] Thus he wrote at the beginning of the book: 'It is the principal aim of the following chapters to prove that this new style, a genuine and adequate style of our century, was achieved by 1914.'[22] And at the end of the book he reaffirmed that 'this new style of the twentieth century . . . because it is a genuine style as opposed to a passing fashion is totalitarian'.[23] The notion of style so 'totalitarian' that no one may opt out of it seems to deprive the word of any meaning. Indeed, Gombrich has argued that we can only recognize style 'against the background of alternative choices'.[24]

With their curious combination of Marxist and Puginian overtones, these arguments were first worked out by Pevsner in the classes he gave at Göttingen University in 1930, where he had been appointed a lecturer the year before. The results were first published in 1931 in the *Göttingische gelehrte Anzeigen*, in a review of the first volume of Le Corbusier's *oeuvre complète*. Having seen the way his mind was working in his articles of the 1920s on Italian painting, his contemporaries cannot have been surprised by the strongly determinist line he took in connection with the Modern Movement. The reason that the review of 1931 did not lead to a book published in Germany a year or so later is the familiar and ominous one consequent upon Hitler's rise to power. As a Jew, Pevsner found it prudent to leave Germany, and he settled in this country in 1934, having given up his lectureship at Göttingen.

Having arrived in a country where the Modern Movement in architecture was not taken very seriously, he undertook to win England to belief in Gropius, while in Germany the absolute archi-tectural norms which he adhered to were being denied by Hitler and his propagandists; for them Modern Architecture was appro-priate enough for factory buildings but not for civic or domestic architecture. This distinction did violence to Pevsner's conception of the modern style as something which ought to be essentially 'totalitarian' and which ought to exercise overriding claims in every kind of situation. In the conservative insular England of 1933, he found another enemy to fight: the view that Modern Architecture was a rootless continental fad fit only as the subject of cartoons in *Punch*. Hence the young Pevsner, whose mission had been rejected in Germany, felt called to continue his work in England by helping it find and appreciate its essence in a collective spirit previously unknown to it. The gospel which he brought with him from Germany was naturalized in England by finding an indigenous ancestry for it. Thus Walter Gropius was cast in the role of the ful-filment of William Morris, and their photographs appear side by side as if in mutual congratulation on the title-page of *Pioneers of the Modern Movement*.

We shall investigate the themes and techniques of *Pioneers of the Modern Movement* from the point of view of the belief first in honesty, secondly in technology, and thirdly in the spirit of youth; finally we shall see how these are all contained within a belief in the

Zeitgeist. The basic concept of honesty is stated clearly in the opening pages, where it is claimed that Victorian design was bad because it was dishonest and made use of what Pevsner loosely refers to in a moralizing Ruskinian way as 'sham materials and sham technique'. This was exactly the reason for which Pugin had condemned Regency design so that, in this sense, he was also a pioneer of the modern movement. However, Pugin had one disqualification: he, unlike Morris, was not a socialist. It is essential to the argument of *Pioneers of the Modern Movement* that modern design, as a constituent of the as yet unrealized essence of modern society, is necessarily socialist. Pevsner proves that Victorian architecture was immoral and dishonest by quoting on the first page of his book the familiar story of how Lord Palmerston persuaded George Gilbert Scott to alter the design of his new Government Offices in Whitehall from Gothic to Classic. 'Against the profound artistic dishonesty which made this comedy possible', writes the disapproving Pevsner, 'the campaign of William Morris's lifetime was directed.'[25] It is therefore ironical that in the 1972–3 *Annual* of the Victorian Society, of which Pevsner was then Chairman, an article on the preservation of the Foreign Office by Scott and M.D. Wyatt observes that:

> The Foreign Office seen in the context of Whitehall and of St. James's Park remains one of the finest government buildings in the world, and must be retained for England as of primary importance to its heritage. . . . We were also disturbed at the dispersal of much of the original furniture, fittings, fireplaces, light fittings etc. . . . There is, throughout the building, a huge collection of pictures, sculpture, furniture, light fittings, fireplaces and fixtures of all sorts, all of great value and interest.[26]

Despite the fact that Morris turns out to have directed his lifetime's campaign against a system which produced a masterpiece of architecture and craftsmanship, Pevsner is still able to maintain in new editions of his book that 'if Morris denounced the social structure of his time so eloquently, his main reason was that it is evidently fatal to art'.[27] And thus, surprisingly, 'Morris is the true prophet of the twentieth century, the father of the Modern Movement.' An essential part of the myth woven around Morris is that he was somehow the first person ever to show an interest in the design of ordinary objects. 'We owe it to him', Pevsner claims, 'that an ordinary man's dwelling-house has once more become a worthy object of the architect's thought, and a chair, a wallpaper, or a vase a worthy object of the artist's imagination.'[28]

But Pevsner's attitude to Morris is ambiguous. Though he is claimed as 'the father of the Modern Movement', it seems that he is not actually a 'pioneer of the Modern Movement' because he did not love the machine. Faith in technology is an essential part of the Zeitgeist Pevsner wishes to establish: 'The true pioneers of the Modern Movement are those who from the outset stood for machine art.'[29] There is much praise of the machine in the early part of the book and of the 'first architects to admire the machine and to understand its essential character'.[30] However, exactly what is meant by 'the machine' and 'machine art' is never defined. How, for example, do we distinguish between a tool and a machine? Does the use of moulds in constructing Jacobean or Adam plaster-work constitute an example, whether good or ill, of the use of the machine? In fact it is clear that what Pevsner is interested in is not so much whether designers make use of what he regards as a machine, but what they say will be the beneficial effects of using the machine. Ironically, Morris, who attacked the machine in his writings, made considerable use of it in practice, whereas designers like Day, Sedding, and Muthesius (whom Pevsner especially admires for their praise of the machine) in fact did not use it. Thus what Pevsner seems to admire is basically a literary, romantic, even sentimental approach to the machine. He does see, however, that 'there is still an immense difference between this hesitating acknowledgement of machinery and the wholehearted welcome which it received in the writings of the leaders of the next generation'. It was in Vienna in the 1890s, in Wagner and Loos, that Pevsner found theorists particularly after his heart – though it is hard to discern any connection with Morris in their opinion that artistic forms must be determined by the material needs of a society which is centred on belief in the machine. Their view is explicitly and admiringly cited by Pevsner. Thus Otto Wagner in 1894 informs us that 'the only possible departure for artistic creation is modern life'; 'all modern forms must be in harmony with . . . the new requirements of our time'; 'nothing that is not practical can be beautiful'. Pevsner finds that 'what is more astonishing' is that Wagner predicted the forms of this new socially responsible and mechanistic architecture when he guessed that it would have 'horizontal lines such as were prevalent in Antiquity, table-like roofs, great simplicity and an energetic exhibition of construction and materials'.[31] But how are horizontal lines necessarily more expressive of 'the new requirements of our time' than vertical lines, and why should a building be better constructed because it makes a feature of exhibiting its construction rather than of not exhibiting it? It is surely clear that all these are aesthetic demands made by people who have already decided what they want buildings to look like, and who then persuade the public to accept them as though they were the inevitable consequence of the facts of modern life and society. Pevsner responded enthusiastically to Wagner's prediction because he thought it foreshadowed the appearance of Bauhaus architecture. He accepts the language of visual form and fashion but defends it only as a social and technological necessity. He praises Loos, for whom ornament was anti-social and immoral, and technology a kind of god. He also seems to support Loos's view that 'the lower the standard of a people, the more lavish are its ornaments'. For Loos it is the engineers who are 'our Hellenes. From them we receive our culture.'

This abandonment of all that has traditionally been understood as culture was taken to an extreme degree in the writings of Frank Lloyd Wright which are approvingly quoted by Pevsner. Wright's manifesto of 1903

> begins straight away with a panegyric on our 'age of steel and steam
> . . . the Machine age, wherein locomotive engines, engines of indus-
> try, engines of light or engines of war or steamships take the place

works of Art took in previous history'. . . . In such an age, the painter or the poet does not count for much. 'Today we have a scientist or an inventor in the place of a Shakespeare or a Dante.' At least, this is what the style of the twentieth century could be like and ought to be like. . . . So Wright's position in 1903 was almost identical with that of the most advanced thinkers on the future of art and architecture today.[32]

We can recognize today what was more difficult to perceive in 1936, that Wright's 'position' was just uncouth and arrogant philistinism. One of the reasons why the blatant crudities that Wright wrote in such great quantity have not been acknowledged for what they are, is that he happened to be an architect of great imagination. His houses were subtle, expensive, romantic: everything we would not expect from his writings. In a word, his buildings had 'style'.

Another architect who argued that there should be no such thing as style in the twentieth century was Berlage. Pevsner summarized him as follows:

> Berlage recommended the architect not to think in terms of style while designing buildings. Thus alone, he said, can real architecture comparable to that of the Middle Ages be created, architecture as a 'pure art of utility'. Such architecture he visualised as '*the* art of the 20th century', and it should be noted that the century to him was to be one of Socialism.[33]

This passage, wherein the minds of Berlage and Pevsner are inextricably involved, contains a remarkable confluence of determinist fallacies. Behind it lies the notion that a new type of man is emerging who has somehow escaped from history and can create a perfect timeless form of building, 'real architecture', which must be totally styleless since style is necessarily transient. It is the belief familiar from Hegelian Marxism that history is moving towards the rebirth of an un-alienated man. We are encouraged to believe in the possibility of this 'real' architecture by the Gothic cathedrals which, in accordance with the views of the French rationalists, are still held up as examples of pure utilitarianism undefiled by stylistic or imaginative genius. This 'real' architecture will also, in some indefinable way, be essentially socialist in character, so as to fit exactly the image of 'real man' as he finally emerges in the twentieth, the 'real', century. A consequence of its socialist character is that it will dominate totally all individual life: it will not be possible to diverge from it since it will be '*the* art of the 20th century'.

This art is born, apparently, of a synthesis between the world of Morris's handicrafts and that of those theorists who preached 'the immense, untried possibilities of machine art'. Pevsner argued that 'The synthesis, in creation as well as in theory, is the work of Walter Gropius (born 1883).'[34] However, to present him as the necessary synthesis, Gropius's history had to be 'tidied up' very considerably by following the distorted account in his book, *The New Architecture and the Bauhaus* (1935). Modern research, particularly by Wolfgang Pehnt,[35] has emphasized what Gropius concealed, that in its early years the Bauhaus was simply an Expressionist art-school.

In our exposition of three of the themes underlying Pevsner's interpretation of modern architecture and design – honesty, technology, and the spirit of youth – we pass now to the third. We find Pevsner evoking in his book the spirit of the 'Youth Movement' which, he felt, lay behind the painting and architecture of the late nineteenth and early twentieth centuries and which presumably accompanied the birth of modern man at the dawn of the new age. The passage in which he first referred to this spirit was prompted by the paintings of Rousseau, and, with its belief in Futurism and 'Vitalism', echoed the clichés of German romanticism from the 1890s to the 1920s:

> But the essential point about [Rousseau], and the whole of the movement which set in about 1890, is that here at last, after a long run of art for art's sake, other qualities than those of purely aesthetic appeal begin to matter. The decrease in aesthetic value is counterbalanced by an increase in *live value*, and that is in our context tantamount to historical value. Rousseau is not as great a painter as Renoir, but he

is an outstanding exponent of a movement which at that time occupied European thought and European feeling far beyond the narrow
world of art: namely the 'Youth Movement' in its widest sense.[36]

The 'Youth Movement' also had something to do with nudism
which was another expression of honesty: 'Fidus . . . has a similar
[i.e. to Hodler] predilection for young and not yet fully developed
bodies, and for allegorical subjects. His part in the history of the
movement is that he links it up with the beginnings of Nudism in
Germany – which is another aspect of the universal Youth
Movement.'[37] Pevsner's unitary approach also allowed him to
equate the Youth Movement with Emery Walker and the English
Private Press movement: 'The Doves Press stands at the beginning
of German twentieth-century printing. Honesty, health, and
straightforwardness became the ideals that replaced the sultry
dreams of Art Nouveau aesthetes. These new ideals led at the same
time to the foundation of the Youth Movement in Germany
(*Wandervogel*, 1901).'[38] Here is a belief that design, which is surely
of its very nature contrived, ought somehow to be 'honest' and
uncontrived. The accompanying faith in 'youth' was also expressed
in the mass youth movements in Germany from the *Wandervogel* in
the 1890s to the Hitler Youth in the 1930s.[39] These all reflected a
belief that the spirit of youth and adventure had some special role
to play in a process of social regeneration. With this in mind we can
now appreciate why, in the final sentence of *The New Architecture
and the Bauhaus* (1935), Gropius supposed that the appeal of the
Modern Movement to the young gave it some unchallengeable
authority: 'The ethical necessity of the New Architecture can no
longer be called in doubt. And the proof of this – if proof were
still needed – is that in all countries Youth has been fired with its
inspiration.'
    Pevsner also found support in England for his belief in youth.
Voysey's wallpapers represented a great leap forward 'into a new
world of light and youth'; indeed, 'It is known that, everywhere in
English cultural life, a longing for fresh air and gaiety expressed itself
at the end of Queen Victoria's reign.'[40] Later he defined a little

more fully what he had in mind by 'fresh air and gaiety': 'the new philosophy of the "Youth Movement", a philosophy of *vitality* and community spirit. Abbotsholme was founded in 1889, Bedales in 1892, the Boy Scouts in 1908.'[41] The faith in youth is especially significant since youth represents unrealized unfulfilled potentiality. 'Vitality' is seen as the opposite of tradition and is believed to be part of the future, struggling to express itself against the burden of the past. This is a straightforward echo of Lethaby, from whom Pevsner quoted several times in *An Enquiry into Industrial Art in England*. In the following highly revealing passage Lethaby had blended the Boy Scout Movement with the Arts and Crafts tradition in a mixture coloured by German theories of the anonymous collective unconscious:

> We must not be content until our railways are as ship-shape as a squadron. What other arts have we that hold the same beauty of efficiency, carried forward in an unconsciously developing tradition? Just two or three occur to me. Simple, well-off housekeeping in the country, with tea in the garden; Boy-scouting, and tennis in flannels. These four seem to me our best forms of modern civilization, and must serve as examples of the sort of spirit in which town improvement must be undertaken.[42]

Pevsner believed that certain artistic forms would have a health-giving effect on us, so that he was able to write of a wardrobe designed by Ambrose Heal for the Paris Exhibition of 1900: 'Plain surfaces of slightly fumed and waxed oak contrast with small panels decorated in pewter and ebony. There are no long curves, the patterns are composed of rectangles and gracefully drawn little flowers. The close atmosphere of medievalism has vanished. Living amongst such objects, *we breathe a healthier air*.'[43] The supposition that naturalness and spontaneity represent an advance over more complex artistic and spiritual states finds further expression in a preference for the improving effects of tea as opposed to alcohol. Pevsner emphasizes that tea is the key drink of the new healthy age – the beverage drunk, presumably, by the members of the universal

Youth Movement – and that the architecture of Mackintosh is a natural reflection of it. He writes of Mackintosh's Cranston Tea-Room in Buchanan Street, Glasgow, of 1897:

> In this tea-room – incidentally the first monument of the new 'tea-room movement' which, in its opposition to the stodgy atmosphere of the public house, is another expression of the universal revival of the health and lightness – the walls are decorated with the same long and graceful lines and the same excessively slim figures which we find in the works of Klimt and his followers.[44]

The belief, false as it turned out, that tea would replace alcohol in the new world and that this change was somehow prefigured in art and architecture, shows how arbitrarily the supporters of this concern for total integration choose a certain kind of art and then fabricate a fictitious society which, in their view, is about to emerge and to which art must be integrated.

Returning to our aim of showing how Pevsner's work is coloured by a holistic method, it is evidently essential to his socio-logically determinist picture of Victorian art that there were no 'cultured and leisurely patrons'[45] – though this is a view which facts simply do not bear out. The Industrial Revolution is thus supposed to have killed off patronage. We are given a rapid summary of its achievements from the 'puddling process', 'the invention of the steam-engine with separate condenser', and the 'screw-steamer', to the 'shuttle drop box' and the 'water-frame for spinning'. 'The immediate consequence of this precipitous development', it is argued, 'was a sudden increase in production, demanding more and more hands, and so leading to an equally fast increase in popu-lation.'[46] Thus 'the consumer had no tradition, no education, and no leisure, and was, like the producer, a victim of this vicious circle'.[47] One of the reasons why men did not break out of this vicious circle was that 'they did not venture to touch the one essen-tial problem, the indissoluble unity of the art of an age and its social system'.[48] Given his holistic approach, Pevsner's lack of enthusiasm for some aspects of Victorian art makes him disapprove of Victorian society, even if it means inventing a whole class of illiterate patrons. He ignores the fact that Morris's achievement was made possible by the Industrial Revolution in that it was supported by the fortune he inherited from his father's mining speculations. Despite the increasing medievalism and elaboration of Morris's decorative designs, Pevsner defends the strange notion of him as a 'Pioneer of the Modern Movement'. He recognizes, none the less, that Morris sometimes fell short of the high ideals that were later to be set by Gropius: 'it must certainly be admitted that, in stained-glass designed by Morris's firm, there is more detail-realism than we can now approve of for ornamental purposes.'[49]

Even Norman Shaw is claimed as a pioneer of the Modern Movement because his work echoes 'so simple, reasonable, undated a style, so much a "no style in particular" (L. Day)[†] that, by following it, Shaw came nearer to the spirit of our century than any Continental architect at that time.'[50] Yet if a thoroughly old-fashioned and conservative Victorian like Shaw could anticipate in his architectural forms the 'spirit of our century', then the argument that those forms are a product of 'the indissoluble unity of the art of an age and its social system' falls to the ground.

Nevertheless architects like Shaw are praised for the following reasons: 'the way for *a future style* in architecture and design was cleared by English artists . . . The part played by England in the growing movement was to maintain and revive wholesome traditions, in order to secure a solid foundation upon which the structure could be built.'[51] This is an art history which disregards the individual circumstances and achievements of individual artists, the alternatives they accepted or rejected, and instead manipulates actors building up to the denouement of a predetermined drama. Works of art are assigned merit in accordance with whether they are prefigurations of a *Zeitgeist* about to be born.

Together with the architect Shaw, certain nineteenth-century painters were praised for having pointed forwards to an as yet unrealized future:

[†] Lewis F. Day (1985–1910), the industrial designer.

Symbolism may be a strength and a weakness – an endeavour towards sanctity or an affectation. Cézanne and van Gogh stand on the one side, Toorop and Khnopff on the other, the former strong, self-disciplined, and exacting, the latter weak, self-indulgent, and relaxing. So the one led into a future of *fulfilment*, that is the establishment of the Modern Movement of the twentieth century, the other into the blind alley of Art Nouveau.[52]

In the language of progressivism 'fulfilment' is a key word. It refers to the spirit (*Geist*) seeking to realize itself in a process of liberation from the shackles of the present. Art Nouveau is censured because 'it is based on individual inventiveness' so that 'a genuine universal style could not therefore spring from it'.[53] Again, the historian's notion of the pre-ordained and prefigurative development takes precedence over what the individual men of the period under discussion actually thought and did. The significance of Art Nouveau is thus thought to lie not in what it was, but what it is supposed to have made possible: 'The new appreciation of decorative art was now established, and the way cleared for the coming development.'[54] In *Pioneers of Modern Design*, published after the war, the account of Art Nouveau was considerably enlarged with references to the Pre-Raphaelites, to Sullivan, and to Gaudí. Bent on showing that architectural forms are always integral to social structure, Pevsner was interested to find that the most extreme statement of Art Nouveau, i.e. in the form which least anticipated Modern Architecture, was to be found in Spain, the country which he took to be the least forward-looking and democratic. He thus argued, in connection with the work of Gaudí in Barcelona, that: 'Thus it cannot be unexpected that Art Nouveau reached its highest achievement in a country marginal to later nineteenth-century developments in art and architecture, and a country in which social conditions had remained wholly unchallenged.'[55] Despite the 'unreformed' social order of England, English artists had nevertheless come close to producing a style which would 'fit' the twentieth century. But this promise was never fulfilled. Disease set in and Pevsner was obliged to look to Germany for the cure. The reasons for England's fall from grace are clear: her love of tradition and her individualism. For neither of these vital, different, yet mutually sustaining characteristics is there room in the new world, in what Pevsner continually describes so selectively as 'our century':

> For various reasons England forfeited her leadership in the shaping of the new style just after 1900, that is, at the very moment when the work of all the pioneers began to converge into one universal movement. One reason was given in Chapter I: the levelling tendency of the coming mass movement – and a true architectural style *is* a mass movement – was too much against the grain of the English character. A similar antipathy prevented the ruthless scrapping of traditions which was essential to the achievement of a style fitting our century.[56]

That final sentence indicates clearly the strength of *Zeitgeist*-worship, of the belief that one must always be in step with the latest moment of the forward-moving trends of the day.

If social structure in England had impeded good design, what of America with its more open and less traditional society? America too, we find, lacked sufficient collectivist spirit so that 'the initiative was confined to a few ingenious architects'.[57] Amongst these was Wright, whose significance is defined as follows: 'To sum up, Frank Lloyd Wright's outstanding importance lies in the fact that nobody else, not even Adolf Loos, had by 1900 come so near to the style of today.'[58] This approach to architectural history seems to imply that chronological progression must mean artistic progress. It is very different from Geoffrey Scott's belief that: 'The values of art do not lie in the sequence but in the individual terms. To Brunelleschi there was no Bramante; his architecture was not Bramante's unachieved, but his own fulfilled.'[59] Pevsner's approach leads to an obsession with what he calls 'the possibility of "misdating"'.[60] This is a clear indication of his belief that it is always essential to be 'up to date' and even to anticipate, where possible, the future. Thus the buildings he singles out for particular praise are not objects of great quality produced by some special imagination, but are buildings that, for better or worse, one can place in the sequence of emergence of the 'modern style'. A building is admirable if an observer sees it as belonging to a date later than that when it was actually constructed. As we have already seen, this is the significance which Pevsner attaches to Wright; it is the same with Tony Garnier, August Endell, and, of course, with Walter Gropius whose pre-First World War factory buildings he praises as representing the 'fulfil-ment of the style of our century' because 'they hide their real dates more effectively than anything we have yet seen'.[61] Yet if interest in art or architecture is supposed to centre on objects which can be misdated because they are 'ahead of their time', there can surely be no logical reason for giving more praise to an object because it looks later than it is, than to an object which looks earlier than it is. There is, of course, no intrinsic reason why we should prefer an object of 1620 which looks thirty years later, to an object of 1650 which looks like one of 1620. But Pevsner is none the less insistent that 'for the historian of architecture, Wright's earlier buildings are more important', because the 'monotonous rhythm of their extended horizontals and their widely projecting roofs have become favour-ite motives of post-war architecture in Europe'.[62] We see here, as we have seen before, that in the final analysis Pevsner's notion of what modern architecture ought to be is entirely visual, a matter of horizontal lines and projecting eaves, a matter of style pure and simple. He is not interested in, or disapproves of, Wright's post-war buildings which have 'become more and more fantastic' and show that 'like Le Corbusier and Picasso, he is a poet of pure form'.[62] The work is disapproved of because its forms are not thought to be socially responsible, and the same is true of much of the art of the period:

> To extol, in the art of Picasso or Kandinsky, their profound self-expression through the medium of abstract shape and colour, shows a wrong or at least onesided interpretation. No doubt many of the abstract painters of today consider self-expression their principal mission; but history will decide against this. Their extreme individ-ualism is of the past, *a reductio ad absurdum* of a conception which had been dominant for more than three hundred years. Only in so far as

their art can be regarded as decoration in the service of architecture, do they work for a new ideal, the ideal of their own century.[63]

This passage shows us how, according to the progressivist view, anything which reminds one 'of the past' is regarded as a vice. The passage did not reappear after the war in *Pioneers of Modern Design*, but an argument present in both books is that the spirit of Gropius's pre-First World War factories was manifested in the large-scale social planning undertaken in Germany immediately after the First World War. He writes of the spirit of these factories that 'we may also recognise it in the sweeping plans for the future layout of whole provinces, which were first made in Germany immediately after the war ("Landesplanung", Ruhr District, Upper Silesia, etc.)'.[64] He argues, furthermore, that 'The profound affinity of this modern enthusiasm for *planning* (architectural as well as political) with the style of Gropius's Fagus factory is evident.' Since what Pevsner particularly admires are horizontal lines and windows that wrap round corners it is hard to see the 'evident' connection with political planning. Pevsner's coupling of Gropius's style with political planning is further evidence of his conviction that everything is and should be expressive of an essence outside art itself.

The emphasis on 'planning' leads us to the peroration of the whole book:

The warm and direct feelings of the great men of the past may have gone; but then the artist who is representative of this century of ours must needs be cold, as he stands for a century cold as steel and glass, a century the precision of which leaves less space for self-expression than did any period before.

However, the great creative brain will find its own way even in times of overpowering collective energy, even with the medium of this new style of the twentieth century which, because it is a genuine style as opposed to a passing fashion, is totalitarian . . . While in the thirteenth century all lines, functional though they were, served the one artistic purpose of pointing heavenwards . . . the glass walls are now clear and without mystery, the steel frame is hard, its expression regardless of otherworldly speculation. It is the creative energy of this world in which we live and work and which we want to master, a world of science and technique, of speed and danger, of hard struggles and no personal security, that is glorified in Gropius's architecture.[65]

This apostrophe of 'danger' and hardness, and this injunction to be 'as cold as steel', cannot but remind us of the Nazi command to be '*zäh wie Leder, hart wie Stahl und schnell wie ein Windhund*' (tough as leather, hard as steel, and swift as a greyhound). It reminds us of the pervasiveness of the collectivist outlook and of its affinities with Bolshevism and National Socialism, with neither of which would Pevsner have wished to identify himself. But on that stark materialist note the book ends: the Brave New World is at hand, a world of violence and inhumanity, a world that has been robbed of all joy, all splendour, all mystery. There, at any rate, *Pioneers of the Modern Movement* ends. But after the Second World War in *Pioneers of Modern Design*, the sentence which ends with the claim that the spirit of the modern world 'is glorified in Gropius's architecture' is immediately followed by a new plea: 'and as long as this is the world and these are its ambitions and problems, the style of Gropius and the other pioneers will be valid'.[66] Written at a time when the Gropius style of 1910 no longer seemed so thrilling to the younger architects as it had in the 1930s, this addition is highly significant. It shows the extent to which Pevsner believed that there was a set of universally acceptable answers to the political and social problems of the twentieth century, and that these were mirrored so absolutely in a particular type of architecture that to question one was to question the other. What Pevsner is effectively proposing is a morally, socially, politically, and artistically cohesive package from which no one must be at liberty to abstain.

There are a number of minor changes to the 1936 text of *Pioneers of the Modern Movement* which reappeared in 1949 as *Pioneers of Modern Design*. For example, in the earlier book the ideals of the English and German Arts and Crafts movements were 'honesty, health, and straightforwardness',[67] whereas in the later book they were 'honesty and saneness'.[68]† Such modifications are trivial and Pevsner himself makes clear in his new post-war Foreword that there is no 'recantation or revision'.[69] Indeed, far from being 'revisionist' the message of the book becomes, as we have seen, more insistent with the passing of time. He reaffirmed after the war, in the face of opposition, that the style of Gropius is still 'valid', and added a sentence which explained that strength and coldness are the virtues of the collectivism which suppresses individuality: 'The architect, to represent this century of ours, must be colder, cold to keep in command of mechanized production, cold to design for the satisfaction of anonymous clients.'[70]

Anonymity had been a key concept in early nineteenth-century German Romanticism where anonymous creation had been emphasized in linguistics and folklore. We have seen the survival of this tradition in the writings of Lethaby, Read, and Richards. It also coloured the first edition of *Pioneers of the Modern Movement*, where the romantic myth of medieval cathedrals as an anonymous building endeavour is used to support the claims of nineteenth-century engineering. Clifton suspension bridge is compared to 'Amiens, Beauvais and Cologne',[71] while of the little-known engineer who designed the Halle des Machines at the Paris Exhibition of 1889, Pevsner writes: 'His name is hardly known to historians of architecture. The healthy state of anonymity, a matter of course in mediaeval building, is preserved here, while it was lost in architecture, owing first to the Renaissance and then to the Romantic conception of the artist and his individual genius.'[72]

The suppression of the individual in favour of the collectivity

---

† Another change is that in the passage which claims that Gropius's architecture, 'because it is a genuine style as opposed to a passing fashion, is totalitarian', the word 'totalitarian' is replaced by 'universal'. It is unnecessary to analyse yet a third presentation of these ideas in the form of Pevsner's book, *The Sources of Modern Architecture and Design*, 1968. In an interesting review of this book, Stanford Anderson wrote of its relation to *Pioneers of the Modern Movement*: 'The changes are not of great significance, the more casual quality of *Sources* and the passing years have only made the underlying Pevsnerian historiography more glaringly weak'. (*Art Bulletin*, liii, June 1971, p. 275.)

which alone has permanent validity is, of course, as characteristic of the political rhetoric of the socialistic and communistic radicalism of the Weimar Republic of Pevsner's young manhood, as it was of the National Socialism which succeeded it. The onslaught on style was necessary to both, because style necessarily implies individual aesthetic choice. This is why Pevsner claimed in 1936 that the modern design which he preferred 'because it is a genuine style as opposed to a passing fashion, is totalitarian'.[†]

In 1936 Pevsner was also carrying out research for yet another book which, in its concern for the creation of an integrated totality, saw artistic design as political commitment. This appeared in 1937 as *An Enquiry into Industrial Art in England*. It is not merely an 'enquiry' but a vigorous manifesto for the adoption by English designers of Bauhaus forms, rather than those which were generally popular in this country between the wars. In his sustained attacks on what he calls 'period imitation', he implied that the modernism he admired was somehow not a period style but a moral imperative beyond the reach of fashion. He was particularly unhappy that modern designers had not yet been able to 'create a style of jewellery really independent of past standards',[73] because anything to do with the past stands condemned for that very fact. In pondering the question, 'How can those basic functions of jewellery be combined

---

[†] The plea for the suppression of the individual which we have noticed in Pevsner's writings was echoed by Mies van der Rohe, whom we have already quoted as arguing that 'the individual is losing significance; his destiny is no longer what interests us', and also by Goebbels who claimed that 'the individual is being dethroned'. With such an outlook it is perhaps not so surprising that Mies van der Rohe was able in 1933 to sign 'a patriotic appeal which Schultze-Naumburg had made as Commissar to the artists, writers and architects of Germany to put their forces behind National Socialism' (S. Moholy-Nagy in *Journal of the Society of Architectural Historians* (U.S.A.), xxiv, Mar. 1965, p. 84). As Professor B. Miller Lane has shown, 'the Nazis exercised control over architectural style not simply because it was the habit of the new regime to regulate public opinion . . . but because they saw architectural styles as symbols of specific political views . . . This belief was not, however, the product of the "totalitarian" structure of the Nazi state. The Nazis inherited a political view of architecture from the Weimar Republic'. (*Architecture and Politics in Germany, 1918–1945*, Harvard U.P., 1968, pp. 2–3.)

with the canons of our modern style?' he is forced to admit that they cannot, 'without deep changes in the universal outlook on life'.[74] These changes are moral, social, and political. They involve, first, sympathy with and belief in the spirit of the age: 'If manufacturers who truly believe in their age will take the risk of pushing a new and unprecedented type of design . . . then success, artistic as well as commercial success, is irresistibly theirs.'[75] No one must ever be allowed to withdraw from this belief in the absolute value of the ideals of the modern world and in their abiding expression in a particular form of modern design: 'Unless a rigid standard of quality and of style – which is, as I shall be showing later, almost the same – is set up and ruthlessly maintained, no success of real consequence will be possible.'[76] Pevsner particularly censured the Exhibition of British Art in Industry, held in 1935 at Burlington House, for its failure to impose this ruthless and rigid uniformity. He quoted with disapproval the comment by the President of the Royal Academy in connection with the Exhibition that 'design might be traditional or modern, if it were original', and also the even more penetrating remark by Goodhart-Rendel: 'New or old in style? It will all soon be old, and neither better nor worse for that.'[77]

One of the reasons why the orthodoxy Pevsner had wished to establish must not be challenged is that it is grounded in a particular morality. This is implicit throughout the book and is sometimes stated directly:

In a cardboard travelling-case made to imitate alligator skin, in a bakelite hairbrush made to imitate enamel – there is something dishonest. A pressed-glass bowl trying to look like crystal, a machine-made coal-scuttle trying to look hand-beaten, machine-made mouldings on furniture, a tricky device to make an electric fire look like a flickering coke fire, a metal bedstead masquerading as wood – all that is immoral. So are sham materials and sham technique. And so is all showy, pompous, blatant design.[78]

A footnote after the words 'sham technique' reads: 'I admit that this principle cannot be pushed to its extreme. If we wanted to be really orthodox we ought to condemn all so-called crystal-glass (as Ruskin did) because it is not true crystal.' But surely it is either a principle or it is not a principle. And if it is not, then it must be a matter of taste. If it is really to be a moral principle rather than an aesthetic preference, then it must be equally immoral for a hand-beaten coal-scuttle to try to look like a machine-made one as for a machine-made scuttle to look hand-beaten. Indeed, if we are to apply the natural law to the art of design it might be immoral to make coal-scuttles at all since they do not exist in nature! Beneath all this lies the praise of the naturalness and authenticity of unalien-ated man completely identified with his society, as against the com-plexity of an art which builds on the interaction between tradition and the imagination of the individual.

Pevsner's insistence on the obligation of every action and every artefact to conform to the universally valid pattern enjoined by the emergent *Zeitgeist* showed itself in his attitude to chocolate boxes. He conducted an inquiry into the artistic taste of chocolate eaters and was not at all pleased by the results. In his view, Cadbury's colourful and picturesque boxes so popular in England, particularly at Christmas, should be abolished in favour of ones that would 'be in harmony with their clean, simple and bright factory buildings, and with their epoch-making garden city . . .' But the English were quite irresponsible in their approach to chocolates, and instead of buying boxes that reminded them of factories chose boxes illustrat-ing 'Venetian gondolas or hunting scenes, for example'. The reasons for Pevsner's disapproval are made clear in his comments on the leading artists who were commissioned by Cadbury's to design Christmas boxes in the 1930s: 'The approach adopted by some of them to the designing of a box for a given commercial article was certainly not the right one. Neither a circus scene nor a still life of fruit has a natural and easily understandable relation to chocolate.'[79] The concern even with so slight a thing as a chocolate box shows the extent to which Pevsner was dominated by his holistic aspira-tion to make everything conform to a single pattern – in this case, an industrial building located outside artistic tradition.

The dependence on moral, political, and social views of

Pevsner's architectural ideal and its universal implications ranging from the design of garden cities to that of coal-scuttles and chocolate boxes, is clear from many passages in, and indeed from the whole tone of, *An Enquiry into Industrial Art in England*. What he proposes is all one package in which, he argues, none of the many topics he discusses should be neglected, 'neither the levelling up of class contrasts nor the raising of standards of design'[80] – note that these two seem somehow to be regarded as identical. The constant reduction in the range of possibilities, the passionate belief in the homogeneous and the anonymous, is given clear expression in the following passage:

> . . . a style of our age must be an unexclusive style, and its merits must be collective merits not distinguishing one individual or one class. It shows at its best in factories, office buildings, blocks of flats, estates of small houses, and buildings for public welfare such as schools, hospitals, swimming pools, etc.[81]

The praise of anonymity, of an 'unexclusive style' with 'collective merits', leaves no room for individual differences since anonymity and conformity go together. Modern design, then, is essentially egalitarian in character exactly as Gothic design had been Roman Catholic for Pugin. It is also, as we saw in *Pioneers of the Modern Movement*, essentially healthy. Its progress was impeded, even in Germany, by imperfectly cleaned teeth: a curious argument proposed by Pevsner on the basis of a questionnaire carried out in 1934 by the 'Health Service of the Museum of Hygiene' in Dresden. The questionnaire showed, amongst other things, that 18.2 per cent of children used 'a family toothbrush'. 'No wonder', Pevsner comments on reporting this fact, 'that in such conditions no sense of beauty and hardly a sense of tidiness can be developed. And no wonder either that the natural longing for beauty, inborn in almost everybody, slakes itself on the cinema, on showy furnishings and "kitschy" pictures in the house and on the portraits of film stars – heroes and heroines of dreams of wish-fulfilment – in the workshops.'[82] The general notion that the forms of modern architecture and design are health-giving leads Pevsner to propose a campaign 'above all for cleaner children and cleaner parents, and for healthier and more modern school buildings'. He equates health with modernity, and sees cleanliness as a restoration of the natural condition as opposed to the complexity of civilization.

What, one may ask, had Pevsner in mind in speaking of this anonymous unexclusive style of our age with its collective merits? One answer lay in the London Underground. He published a number of articles in the 1930s (e.g. on Mackmurdo in 1938, and Walton in 1939) which culminated in 'Patient Progress; the Life Work of Frank Pick' in 1942.[83] His belief that the spirit of the age is more important than its individual manifestations and the consequent preoccupation with so-called 'misdateable' buildings which look as though they were designed later than they really were, led him to elevate to key importance architects of slender talents like Mackmurdo and George Walton. The latter was assistant architect and designer to the Central Liquor Traffic Control Board which guarded the nationalized pubs of Scotland; of him Pevsner went so far as to claim that: 'Walton, during the years from 1895 to 1905, was one of the most brilliant of that group of British architect-designers who progressed beyond Morris towards a new style of the twentieth century.'[84]

This belief in the architecture of collective, not individual, merit culminated in Pevsner's admiration for Frank Pick who rose from being Traffic Development Officer of the Underground Electric Railways in 1909, to become Commercial Manager in 1912, and finally Vice-Chairman of the London Passenger Transport Board in 1933. As an indication of Pick's beneficent influence, Pevsner shows us how he replaced designs such as that by S.A. Heaps for Brent Station on the Edgware extension, with ones like Charles Holden's Clapham South Station on the Morden extension. Looking at the two stations today from a point fifty years later, there must be many who prefer the quiet elegance of Brent Station, with its welcoming Palladian colonnade, to the hostile brutality of Clapham South. But Pevsner argues that 'the L.P.T.B. stands for an architecture unequalled by transport design in any other metropolis and [that] it has by means of its buildings and publicity become the most efficacious centre of visual education in England.'[85] To prove the point we are shown photographs ranging from the ventilation tower at the Bounds Green station to the locker room at the Acton Works. Pevsner believes that people will enjoy the new bus shelters so much that they will want their own homes to assume the features of bus shelters: 'Those who have experienced the functional advantages of these shelters, the advantages of so much glass and so little in the way of roof support, will be prepared to welcome something of the same kind at home.'[86] Pevsner's collectivist view, coupled with his belief that the *Zeitgeist* has its seat in technology, prevented him from having sympathy with an individual desire for a pleasing domestic environment. Indeed, there is no room for privacy in the new world evoked in these pages. The argument throughout the article is the familiar one that there is something particularly beneficial and improving about architecture from which every trace of ornament, every echo of association, have been eliminated and which has thereby become 'honest', uncontrived, and authentic. Thus the Sudbury Town Station on the South Harrow–Uxbridge line, opened in 1931, is praised for 'telling in its honest exterior that it is not intended to be more than a seemly casing for certain traffic functions'.[87] Not thus was the Euston Propylaeum conceived, the finest railway building of all!

Pick was an earnest and skilful proselytizer, an 'educationalist' as Pevsner calls him, a Lord Reith of the railways. His mission involved the belief that modern design was a necessary part of the new society organized around the technological progress to which all else must be subordinated. At the Charing Cross Booking Hall he organized exhibitions on subjects such as the working of the Milk Marketing Board, the G.P.O., the evening classes of the L.C.C., the *News Chronicle* Better Schools Competition, and the Highway Code. As a consequence, Pevsner regards Pick as a modern counterpart of Lorenzo the Magnificent! Indeed he is yet more satisfactory than Lorenzo de'Medici because the object of Lorenzo's patronage was 'personal enjoyment'. 'No,' Pevsner writes, 'if a Lorenzo can be conceived nowadays, it can only be in terms of big business or big administration, in terms of no leisure and no private glamour.'[88]

Here, at last, we have a clear exposition of why Pevsner has spent so long extolling the work of Frank Pick. The preoccupation with the anonymous collective forces associated with technology and large bureaucratic organizations has led to a position where all one can do is to admire a man like Pick for whom, as Pevsner believes, 'art was always a means to an end'. Both men saw architecture and design as an anonymous, instrumental, mechanical service consecrated to 'community need' as defined by planners, civil servants, and social scientists, though not by the individuals who live in the community. Once more we see Pevsner's postulates: first, that particular architectural or artistic forms are always integral to particular political and social orders; secondly, that architecture is the effective instrument for the realization of the good society; and thirdly, that architects are the right guides and promulgators of social and political ideals.

The notion of architecture as an anonymous mechanical service was anticipated by Pugin in his argument that '*Every building that is treated naturally, without disguise or concealment, cannot fail to look well*',[89] and accounts for our being invited to admire the locker room at the Acton Works of the London Passenger Transport Board. This denial of the role of the architect to raise our spirits, this view that what he does is not the result of education, taste, and imagination but that he is merely the vehicle through which a material problem is resolved with what Pugin calls a 'natural' answer, is ultimately degrading in its 'lowest common denominator' conception of man and his needs. The theme re-emerged as the conclusion of Pevsner's *Outline of European Architecture*, first published in 1943. 'The new Maecenas', according to Pevsner, 'is an administrator, a worker himself, with a house not much bigger than yours and mine, a cottage in the country, and a car far from spectacular.' He will be concerned not with the human being as an individual, but with humanity *en masse*: thus everything 'designed nowadays serves masses and not individuals. Must not therefore our style be one adapted to mass production, not only in the sense of production in masses but also for masses?' The deliberate lowering of sights and elimination of all refined achievement which this outlook implies is not only recognized but positively welcomed: 'Granted that this new style often looks rather forbidding and seems to lack human warmth. But is not the same true of contemporary life? Here, too, amenities to which we have been used are being replaced by something more exacting and more elementary.'[90]

In conclusion we may define the substantive views expressed by Pevsner as follows: praise of industrialism while disliking capitalism; desire for egalitarian uniformity; dislike of any avowal of aesthetic criteria; belief in 'Hardness' and in 'Honesty' with nothing deliberately aiming at beauty. The brutalism which underlies this undoubtedly owes something to the Bolshevik language current in certain artistic and political circles in Europe in the early 1920s.

3. 'Historicism'

We will not have a complete picture of the history and aims of what Pevsner understands by modern architecture unless we investigate his use of the word 'historicism'. The word is given prominent treatment in the important penultimate chapter of *An Outline of European Architecture*, called 'The Romantic Movement, Historicism, and the Beginning of the Modern Movement, 1760–1914'. The wide variety of topics included in this long title are yoked together in the way with which *Pioneers of the Modern Movement* familiarized us seven years earlier: by making Gropius the synthesis of conflicting traditions. The choice of a starting date is equally odd, since the crucial years for the development of neo-classicism were the 1740s and 1750s. In this chapter, 'historicism' is used as a pejorative term to denote the architecture of the nineteenth century, though not of the eighteenth.

Modern philosophers, historians, and sociologists have given a number of complex and subtle meanings to the term 'historicism'.

However, whether they approve of it like Mannheim, or disapprove of it like Popper, they are in general agreement that historicism encourages moral relativism because of its belief that the spirit has a totally new and homogenous expression in each epoch, which thereby renders obsolete the cultural, religious, moral, and political patterns of previous epochs. Spurning the interpretations of historicism by the philosophers and sociologists who have invented and popularized the term, Pevsner uses it, generally in a condemnatory sense, simply to refer to those who allow themselves to be influenced by past styles. If the obligation of an architect is to express his age, and the defining features of his age are outside architectural traditions and style, lying in technology and political belief, then an architect who adheres to a style cultivated in another, any other, period must be castigated as retrograde. Curiously, this applies only to the nineteenth and twentieth centuries: he does not refer to the Renaissance as historicist. He is puzzled by the fact that Gropius did not emerge in 1800 rather than waiting till 1900, and asks, 'Why was it then that a hundred years had to pass before an original "modern" style was really accepted? . . . [particularly since] such a lack of self-confidence is the last thing one would expect from an epoch so independent in commerce, industry, and engineering.' His surprise is a logical consequence of the expectation that the *Zeitgeist* should be expressed uniformly and totally throughout all the activities of an age. The passage from *An Outline of European Architecture* from which we have just been quoting continues:

It is the things of the spirit in which the Victorian age lacked vigour and courage. Standards in architecture were the first to go; for while a poet and a painter can forget about their age and be great in the solitude of their study and studio, an architect cannot exist in opposition to society . . . Moreover, the iron master and mill-owner, as a rule self-made men of no education, felt no longer bound by one particular accepted taste as the gentleman had been who was brought up to believe in the rule of taste. It would have been bad manners to build against it. Hence the only slightly varied uniformity of the

English eighteenth-century house. The new manufacturer had no manners, and he was a convinced individualist. If, for whatever reasons, he liked a style in architecture, then there was nothing to prevent him from having his way and getting a house or a factory or an office building or a club in that style.

. . . it was a grave symptom of a diseased century that architects were satisfied to be storytellers instead of artists. But then the painters were no better. They too, to be successful, had to tell stories or render objects from nature with scientific accuracy.

Thus by 1830 we find a most alarming social and aesthetic situation in architecture. Architects believed that anything created by the pre-industrial centuries must of necessity be better than anything made to express the character of their own era. Architects' clients had lost all aesthetic susceptibilities, and wanted other than aesthetic qualities to approve of a building.[91]

Here we are given to understand that early nineteenth-century architects went astray because they did not wish to 'express the character of their own era'. The word 'aesthetic' in this context seems to mean nothing more than expressing one's age, while those who do not accept the *Zeitgeist* are anomalies. The view of cultural history as an account of a completely coherent pattern formed around an essence or spirit encourages him to explain away what he understands by 'historicism' as a socially determined force. It may be from his friend James Richards that he derived the idea, expressed by Richards in *An Introduction to Modern Architecture* (1940), that the interest in a variety of earlier styles was a consequence of the break-up of an aristocratic social order and of the emergence of uneducated patrons. We have only to look at two pioneer buildings in exotic styles, Strawberry Hill built for Horace Walpole and the Brighton Pavilion for the Prince Regent, to see how far this view is from the truth. To support the argument that since 'historicism' has a bad influence on style it must have been developed by bad people, Pevsner was forced to invent a whole class of crude middle-class patrons, captains of industry with coarse clothes, bad manners, and loud accents, roaming offensively about

Victorian England, throwing their money about commissioning bog-oak chairs and Butterfield churches. However, in his recent book on Butterfield, Paul Thompson has shown that:

> It was not the new middle class, the philistine industrialists, who were the influential patrons of mid-nineteenth century architecture, but the old aristocracy. It is difficult to think of a single building commissioned by a manufacturer which was crucial to the development of the High Victorian style. Certainly Samuel Sanders Teulon, who was probably the most outrageously 'ugly' architect of the period, relied almost entirely on an aristocratic clientele. Butterfield himself scarcely received a single commission from a manufacturer.[92]

With the launching of the *Buildings of England* series in 1951, Pevsner had to decide how he would deal with modern buildings that made use of 'period imitation'. Not surprisingly, he decided that if twentieth-century 'historicist' buildings other than those in the Gropius manner had to be mentioned, their patrons and architects should be severely admonished. This procedure confers on the series not only Pevsner's unique erudition, but also his distinctive progressivist aesthetic view. The following quotation from the *London and Westminster* volume may be regarded as characteristic:

> ... it ought to be recorded first that the neo-classical, neo-Georgian spectre is even now not yet laid. In no other capital known to me would it be possible to see major buildings still going up which are so hopelessly out of touch with the C20 ... Obviously the idea of security has here been taken to mean the old adage 'What was good enough for my father is good enough for me', and enterprise and courage stand for nothing.[93]

The principle applied to the architectural tradition of Great Britain is the belief explicitly stated in *The Leaves of Southwell* that 'a spirit of the age, operating in art as well as politics ... works changes in style and outlook, and the man of genius is not he who tries to shake off its bonds, but he to whom it is given to express it in the most powerful form.' Thus the reason why no one is allowed to question the current orthodoxies in 1970 is that they *are* the current orthodoxies; thus, too, Pevsner will not accept that it might take 'enterprise and courage' for a man to assert that he would continue to uphold the standards which were accepted in the past, despite living in an age which worshipped novelty for its own sake or as a parallel to industrial innovation. Pevsner does not find such dissent from the prevailing orthodoxy merely reprehensible, but even beyond his understanding. Of various post-Second World War London buildings of which he disapproves he writes, for example: 'almost beyond comprehension', 'incredibly reactionary', 'almost unbelievable for its date', 'almost grotesquely reactionary', 'reactionary beyond belief . . . inscrutable to a visitor from abroad . . .'.[94]

The observations we have briefly made of the *Buildings of England* are obviously not intended as an assessment of the general importance of the series. As an amazing triumph of energy, productiveness, and erudition unequalled in English architectural history, they represent probably the greatest achievement of a great scholar, and will remain of continuing use and value for the foreseeable future. Nevertheless, they bear the imprint of the doctrine that with the birth of truly modern man history has at last been superseded and no one should ever wish to look over his shoulder again.[†] In 1961 Pevsner went even further and extended the ban on 'historicism' to modern architecture as well. Thus it became wrong for an architect to look over his shoulder not merely at 'the neo-classical, neo-Georgian spectre', but also at modern architecture itself. This line, first published in 1961 in an article called 'The Return of Historicism', was an extreme logical extension of the plea he had been making in the 1930s and 1940s for an architecture which must owe absolutely nothing to anything that had gone before it. The new doctrine was proclaimed first in a lecture at the Royal Institute

---

[†] The doctrine is maintained in some of the volumes of *The Buildings of England* series written by Pevsner's collaborators. For example, Ian Nairn, deeply worried by the architecture of Bailiffscourt in Sussex designed by Amyas Phillips in 1935, claims that 'it poses a moral problem which is not at all simple' (Sussex, 1965, p. 98.)

of British Architects in 1961; then it was printed in the *R.I.B.A. Journal* in April 1961; it reached a wider public in the form of a talk given over the wireless in December 1966 which was printed in the *Listener* in December 1966 and January 1967; finally the text of the R.I.B.A. lecture was reprinted in 1968 in Volume II of his *Studies in Art, Architecture and Design*.

The message of 'The Return of Historicism' is stated as follows: 'The principal purpose of this paper is to draw attention to what I regard as an alarming recent phenomenon. It is what can only be called a return of Historicism.' He then goes on to define his own interpretation of this word more clearly than he had done in *An Outline of European Architecture*: 'Historicism is the belief in the power of history to such a degree as to choke original action and replace it by action which is inspired by period precedent. . . . That this kind of historicism was the almost universal trend in architecture [i.e. in the nineteenth century] I need not emphasise.'[95] When Pevsner writes damningly of 'period precedent' he does not merely mean the world of fans and crinolines which 'period' usually implies, but he means any period, even last week. Thus what worries him 'is the imitation of, or inspiration by, much more recent styles, styles which had never previously been revived. Of course, all reviving of styles of the past is a sign of weakness, because in revivals independent thinking and feeling matters less than the choice of patterns.'[96] This passage, which reads like the polemics of a young Italian Futurist in 1914, implies a condemnation of most Western architecture from the first century B.C. to about 1940, based as it was, directly or indirectly, on the classical language established by the Greeks. It enjoins on human beings a continuous rejection of all that has been achieved in the past, and a continuous process of innovation in conformity with the eternally changing *Zeitgeist* and its technological accompaniment. Of course, unlike the Futurist he does not really attempt to put it into practice. He allows Palladio to be inspired by the antique without condemning him as 'historicist'; he allows Scamozzi and also Adam to imitate Palladio, but it is doubtful whether he would grant the same permission to an architect of the nineteenth century, and certain that he has not granted it to one of the twentieth-century – Lutyens, for example. And in the course of this article we learn that he will not allow Howell to be inspired by Rietveld or Gaudí, Utzon by Finsterlin, Saarinen by Behrens, Ungers by Mies van der Rohe, Aalto by Haering, Stone by Perret, Matthes by Le Corbusier. Each man must approach every problem with a mind that is a *tabula rasa*; he must have no cultural expectations or assumptions, no idea of what he wants his artefacts to look like; the form of his buildings must be dictated entirely by their function. Like Mr. Gradgrind, Pevsner is insistent that every feature of every building must have a tangible material use, and he emphasizes that in attacking buildings he is 'trying in this paper always to stop short, where shapes and forms of the kind I am concerned with have a functional justification'.[97] It is the old argument from Pugin of 'convenience, construction, or propriety' and it allows its user to proceed in utter freedom: thus for Pugin it was somehow able to justify the spire but not the portico; for Pevsner it can justify the glazed spiral staircases at either end of Gropius's Administrative Office Building at the Werkbund Exhibition of 1914, but not Johansen's circular American Embassy at Dublin of 1959. What, however, can be the functional justification of wrapping a glass wall round the exposed spiral staircases at the Werkbund building? The only answer is that it has an aesthetic justification. How far the result is aesthetically pleasing will naturally always be a matter for debate, and in the process of assessing Gropius's success one will naturally want to draw comparisons with the use other architects have made of spiral staircases and of glass. What is impossible is that we should feel a moral obligation to prefer Gropius's solution on the spurious argument contained in his own claim that 'the ethical necessity of the New Architecture can no longer be called in doubt'.

In 1963 Pevsner reiterated his interpretation of historicism at a symposium which was published under the title, *Historismus und bildende Kunst, Vorträge und Diskussion im Oktober 1963 in München und Schloss Anif* (Munich, 1965). His misuse of the word 'historicism' so as to mean merely 'period imitation' in the arts, and his consequent failure to recognize that he is himself a historicist in the sense defined by Popper and Mannheim, is made clear in his belief that each epoch, century, or decade has a style which is 'legitimate'[98] and that the role of the individual designer is to do justice to his own time ('der eigenen Zeit gerecht zu werden').[99] He speaks of 'the difficulty of doing justice to one's own time so long as one is convinced of the superiority of a style of the past or of the impossibility of emancipating oneself from the forms of the past.' The view that the ideas and forms of past periods are continually being rendered obsolete and out of date by the new 'essences' of new ages is precisely that which Popper had in mind when he wrote in *The Poverty of Historicism*: 'Every version of historicism expresses the feeling of being swept into the future by irresistible forces', and 'historicism claims that nothing is of greater moment than the emergence of a really new period'.[100] For Popper, historicism is 'the view that the story of mankind has a plot, and that if we can succeed in unravelling this plot we shall hold the key to the future'.[101] Looking back in the 1970s on the impact of *The Poverty of Historicism*, he wrote: 'It was only after the publication of my book that I realised how great the influence of historicism still was in the English-speaking world. It was great in politics, but greater still in art and music, where a completely senseless idea of progress and novelty played a most destructive part.'[102] Gombrich has described the impact of attending in 1936 a seminar at which Popper presented the ideas on historicism which he was to publish in 1944–5. 'This deadly analysis', Gombrich writes, 'of all forms of social determinism derived its urgency from the menace of totalitarian philosophies which nobody at that time could forget for a moment.' He tells us that 'I had become increasingly sceptical of . . . Neo-Hegelian *Geistesgeschichte* and Neo-Marxist Sociologism. This scepticism was not very popular with some continental colleagues, proud of being in the possession of a key that revealed the "essence" of past ages.'[103]

Pevsner's outlook is historicist in precisely the Popperian sense. It is holistic and preoccupied with the future. He believes that art is and should be a product of the economic, social, and political conditions under which it is created; he believes that there is such a thing as the essence of an age, and that the common essence is more important than its individual manifestations; he has accordingly discerned the political and social norms of the twentieth century, and insists that art and architecture must be subordinated to them. Consequently he can and does insist that he knows what will and must be the architectural expression of the age.[†]

[†] In other words, 'unless a further levelling of social differences takes place in this country, no steady development towards the aims of the Modern Movement is possible.'

. . . seeing the natural instability of our customers and opinions, I have often thought, that even good Authors, doe ill, and take a wrong course, wilfully to opinionate themselves about framing a constant and solide contexture of us. They chuse an universall ayre, and following that image, range and interpret all a man's actions . . . *There is nothing I so hardly beleeve to be in man as constancie, and nothing so easie to be found in him, as inconstancy.*

Montaigne's *Essays*, translated by J. Florio, 1928 edn., vol. ii, pp. 7–8.

Conclusion

In outlining the development of an intellectual outlook which has much in common with what Sir Herbert Butterfield called the 'whig' and Sir Karl Popper the 'historicist' interpretation of history, it may have become clear that the assumptions associated with this outlook, as expressed in architectural history, have not been subject to the kind of rigorous historiographical analysis which has been applied since the 1930s to the study of history itself. It seems that no one with a proper training in philosophy, intellectual history, religion, or the social sciences has turned a critical eye on architectural history. Architectural historians have consequently found it easy to fall back on the belief in a unitary, all-pervasive *Zeitgeist*. One important reason for this is that modern art history began in the nineteenth century as a by-product of history and the philosophy of culture in Germany; the rapid growth of popular Marxist sociology, which has a similar intellectual origin, has also played an influential role. Thus everything is seen as a 'reflection' of something else – the economic structure, the spirit of the age, the prevailing theology, and so on. There is also an evolutionary assumption that in each epoch a new economic structure or a new *Zeitgeist* is 'struggling to be born'. It thus becomes the obligation of the creative spirits, be they poets, architects, or whatever, to 'express' that new nascent spirit. To express an antiquated *Zeitgeist* is to be condemned as a poor artist or architect.

But it is man, creative, mysterious, and unpredictable, who is the proper subject of the historian, not the subterranean collective urges of the spirit of the age or of the 'needs' of an as yet nonexistent society. The 'historicist' view is, however, very pervasive so that it is not difficult to detect, for example, in Hugh Honour's otherwise lucid and beautiful book on *Neo-Classicism* (1968) an essentially historicist belief in the absolute value of novelty which enables us to recognize the establishment of a new independent and consistent epoch, and the accompanying assumption that it is not only possible but also desirable to eliminate tradition. He proposes the entirely false view that it was *c.* 1800 that 'the age of historical revivalism had begun'. He then claims that this reduced subsequent art to an affair of revivalism and the devaluation of symbols by stifling all the ceaseless novelty and freshness which would otherwise have been produced. Regarding this devalued art as integral to the political situation of the day, and disapproving of Napoleon, he also sees this artistic debasement as a moral debasement. The same is true of the continuation of the classical tradition in the twentieth century, which he condemns as 'the embodiment of the most reactionary of political programmes' spawning a 'bastard progeny [which] looms large in the perspective of history'.[1]

The attitudes of different historians to the architecture of Sir Edwin Lutyens are always a revealing indication of the extent to which they have assumed, probably unconsciously, a Hegelian holistic outlook. Lutyens was one of the two or three most brilliant and successful architects England has ever produced, yet he completely ignored all the current orthodoxies and conventions which most modern critics tend to suppose will necessarily be reflected in twentieth-century culture. Thus even Professor Henry-Russell Hitchcock, whose work does not usually reveal a belief in the normative claims of the *Zeitgeist*, was reduced to writing the following palpably empty sentence about Lutyens: 'Lutyens, one feels, in a different time and place – a generation earlier in England, say, or a generation later – might have been a greater architect.'[2]

So out of date, so unexpressive of the *Zeitgeist*, was Lutyens that Professor Pevsner fails to mention him at all in *An Outline of European Architecture*. His very existence is not so much as hinted at: 'For the next forty years, the first forty of our century, no English name need here be mentioned.'[3] It is like one of those Russian Communist photographs from which the presence of some politically unacceptable figure has been skilfully eliminated. The reason for the omission of Lutyens is the familiar historicist, Hegelian belief that each age in history must have its own totally consistent pattern which in turn will be replaced by the pattern of the next age moving forwards in a great plan of development.

To the perceptive historian in the nineteenth century the large and individual genius of Michelangelo posed something of the same problem that Lutyens does to modern historians: his spectacular achievement did not 'fit' the current conceptions of what the spirit of the Renaissance was or ought to have been. Thus Jacob Burckhardt, writing in 1867 of Michelangelo's Laurentian Library in his *History of the Renaissance in Italy*, was forced to admit that for him this was just 'an incomprehensible joke of the great master'.[4] But he did not for one moment pretend that, because it did not happen to 'express the spirit of the age', there was no such thing as the Laurentian Library.

Like Burckhardt, we must accept humbly that we do not know all the answers to the problems with which human nature confronts us. What we have seen in this book is the effect of historicism in providing short cuts to the solution of the very complicated problems presented by the relationship between architecture and society. Our conclusion is that an art-historical belief in the all-dominating *Zeitgeist*, combined with a historicist emphasis on progress and the necessary superiority of novelty, has come dangerously close to undermining, on the one hand, our appreciation of the imaginative genius of the individual and, on the other, the importance of artistic tradition.

References

Note: The place of publication is London, unless otherwise stated.
A date in parentheses is that of the first edition

Introduction

1. A.W.N. Pugin, *The True Principles of Pointed or Christian Architecture*, 1841, p. 1.
2. S. Giedion, *Space, Time and Architecture, the Growth of a New Tradition* (1941), 5th edn., Oxford University Press, 1971, p. 705.
3. N. Pevsner, *An Enquiry into Industrial Art in England*, Cambridge, 1937, p. 11.
4. H. Read, *Anarchy and Order, Essays in Politics* (1954), Unitarian Universalist Association, Boston, 1971, pp. 73 and 76.
5. K. Popper, *The Open Society and its Enemies*, 2 vols., 1945, vol. ii, p. 256.
6. N. Pevsner, *The Buildings of England, Staffordshire*, 1974, p. 215.
7. E. Viollet-le-Duc, *Entretiens sur l'architecture*, issued in separate parts, Paris, 1858–72, trans. B. Bucknall as *Discourses on Architecture*, 2 vols., Boston, 1889; reprinted London 1959, vol. i, p. 448.
8. J. Summerson, 'The Case for a Theory of Modern Architecture', *R.I.B.A. Journal*, lxiv, 1957, pp. 309–10.
9. Pevsner, *An Enquiry* p. 202.
10. L. Benevolo, *History of Modern Architecture*, 1971, p. 375.
11. L. Martin, 'Architects' approach to Architecture', *R.I.B.A. Journal*, lxxiv, 1967, p. 191.
12. See R. Banham, 'The New Brutalism', *Architectural Review*, cxviii, Dec. 1955, p. 358.
13. M. Girouard, 'The Outside Story', *Times Literary Supplement*, 23 Feb. 1973, p. 202.
14. A. Pope, *Epistle to Lord Burlington of the use of Riches*, line 36.
15. R. Macleod, *Style and Society, Architectural Ideology in Britain, 1835–1914*, 1971, p. 58.
16. *Ibid.*, p. 136.

129

17. A.W.N. Pugin, *An Apology for the Revival of Christian Architecture in England*, 1843, p. 44.
18. J. Ruskin, *The Stones of Venice*, vol. iii, 1853, chap. II, §4.
19. J. Stirling, *Buildings and Projects, 1950–1974*, 1975, p. 14.
20. In a lecture given at Zurich in 1934 and reprinted in *Marcel Breuer, Buildings and Projects, 1921–1961*, 1962, p. 261.
21. W.R. Lethaby, *Form in Civilisation* (1922), 2nd edn., Oxford, 1957, p. 59.
22. W.R. Lethaby, *Architecture, an Introduction to the History and Theory of the Art of Building* (1911), reprinted 1919, p. 207.
23. S. Giedion, *op. cit.*, p. xxxiii.
24. N. Pevsner, *Pioneers of the Modern Movement*, 1936, pp. 110–11.

Part I. The Theme in the Nineteenth Century

1. Pugin, *An Apology*, pp. 24–5.
2. W. Gropius, *The New Architecture and the Bauhaus*, trans. P.M. Shand 1935, p. 80.
3. F.R. Leavis, *Nor Shall my Sword, Discourses on Pluralism, Compassion and Social Hope*, 1972, p. 24 and elsewhere.
4. Pugin, *Contrasts*, 1836, p. 15
5. Pugin, *The True Principles*, p. 9.
6. Pugin, *Ibid.*, pp. 44–5.
7. *Ibid.*, p. 65.
8. P.B. Stanton, 'Pugin: Principles of Design *versus* Revivalism', *Journal of the Society of Architectural Historians* (U.S.A.), xiii, Oct. 1954, pp. 20–5.
9. Pugin, *The True Principles*, p. 57.
10. Pugin, *An Apology*, p. 10.
11. Pugin, *The True Principles*, pp. 62–3.
12. Pugin, *Contrasts*, p. 31.
13. Pugin, *An Apology*, p. 6.
14. *The Collected Ghost Stories of M.R. James*, 1831, p. 418.
15. Pugin, *An Apology*, p. 11.
16. *Ibid.*, p. 15.
17. *Ibid.*, p. 39.
18. J. Summerson, 'Viollet-le-Duc and the Rational Point of View', *Heavenly Mansions*, 1949, p. 158.
19. Viollet-le-Duc, *Discourses*, vol. i, p. 9.
20. *Ibid.*, p. 10.
21. *Ibid.*, p. 11.
22. *Ibid.*, p. 188.
23. *Ibid.*, pp. 76–7.

24. *Ibid.*, p. 177.
25. *Ibid.*, p. 180.
26. *Ibid.*, pp. 180–1.
27. *Ibid.*, p. 281.
28. *Ibid.*, p. 186.
29. *Ibid.*, p. 237.
30. *Ibid.*, p. 448.
31. *Ibid.*, p. 451.
32. *Ibid.*, pp. 206–7.
33. *Ibid.*, pp. 236–7.
34. *Ibid.*, pp. 237–8.
35. *Ibid.*, p. 304.
36. *Ibid.*, p. 246.
37. E. Viollet-le-Duc, *L'Art russe, ses origines, ses éléments constituifs, son apogée, son avenir*, Paris, 1877, p. 257. My translation.

Part II. The Theme in the Twentieth Century

1. J.M. Richards, *An Introduction to Modern Architecture*, 1940, p. 119.
2. Macleod, *op. cit.*, p. 7.
3. Lethaby, *Architecture*, pp. 205–7.
4. G.D.S. Henderson, *Gothic*, 1967, p. 19.
5. J. Harvey, *The Mediaeval Architect*, 1972, p. 228.
6. *Ibid.*, p. 230.
7. Lethaby, *Architecture*, p. 230.
8. *Ibid.*, p. 232.
9. Henderson, *op. cit.*, pp. 31 and 33.
10. Lethaby, *Form in Civilisation*, p. 9.
11. Lethaby, *Architecture*, p. 242.
12. *Ibid.*, p. 249.
13. P.C. Johnson, *Mies van der Rohe,* Museum of Modern Art, New York (1947), 2nd edn., 1953, pp. 188–9.
14. *Ibid.*, pp. 191–2.
15. Le Corbusier, *Towards a New Architecture*, trans. F. Etchells 1927, new edn., 1946, p. 10.
16. Lethaby, *Form in Civilisation*, p. 33.
17. Le Corbusier, *op. cit.*, p. 13.
18. *Ibid.*, p. 17.
19. *Ibid.*, p. 150.
20. *Ibid.*, p. 203.
21. *Ibid.*, p. 26.

22. *Ibid.*, p. 32. My italics.
23. *Ibid.*, p. 115.
24. *Ibid.*, p. 114.
25. B. Taut, *Modern Architecture*, 1929, p. 9.
26. Le Corbusier and P. Jeanneret, *Œuvre complète de 1929–34*, Zurich, 1935, p. 24.
27. Taut, *op. cit.*, p. 169.
28. *Ibid.*, p. 171.
29. H. Read, *Art and Industry*, 1934, pp. 2–3.
30. *Ibid.*, p. 11.
31. *Ibid.*, p. 17.
32. *Ibid.*, p. 123.
33. Read, *Anarchy and Order*, p. 79.
34. *Ibid.*, pp. 87–8.
35. A. Blunt, 'Art under Capitalism and Socialism', *The Mind in Chains: Socialism and the Cultural Revolution*, ed. C.D. Lewis, 1937, p. 108.
36. *Ibid.*, pp. 116–19.
37. J.L. Martin *et al.*, *Circle International Survey of Constructive Art,* 1937, p. v.
38. *Ibid.*, pp. 1–2.
39. *Ibid.*, p. 9.
40. *Ibid.*, p. 54.
41. *Ibid.*, p. 75.
42. *Ibid.*, p. 111.
43. *Ibid.*, p. 71.
44. *Ibid.*, p. 123.
45. *Ibid.*, p. 264.
46. H. Butterfield, *Christianity and History*, 1949, p. 6.
47. L. Mumford, *The Culture of Cities* (1938), 1940, p. 515.
48. Martin *et al.*, *op. cit.*, pp. 184–5.
49. *Ibid.*, p. 186.
50. *Ibid.*, p. 187.
51. *Ibid.*, p. 188.
52. *Ibid.*, p. 189.
53. Richards, *op. cit.*, p. 15.
54. *Ibid.*, p. 17.
55. *Ibid.*, p. 23.
56. *Ibid.*, p. 33.
57. *Ibid.*, p. 25.
58. H.S. Goodhart-Rendel in a lecture of 1948 published in *Victorian Architecture* ed. P. Ferriday, 1963, p. 83.
59. Richards, *op. cit.*, p. 56.
60. *Ibid.*, p. 57.
61. Giedion, *op. cit.*, p. vii.

62. *Ibid.*, p. vi.
63. K. Popper, *Conjectures and Refutations, The Growth of Scientific Knowledge,* 1963, p. 342.
64. Giedion, *op. cit.*, p. xxxiii.
65. *Ibid.*, p. xliii.
66. *Ibid.*, p. vi.
67. *Ibid.*, p. xxxvii.
68. See R.V. Scruton, 'Architectural Aesthetics', *The British Journal of Aesthetics,* xiii, Autumn 1973, pp. 333–4.
69. Giedion, *op. cit.*, p. 828.
70. *Ibid.*, p. 817.
71. *Ibid.*, pp. 5–6.
72. *Ibid.*, pp. 19–20.
73. J. Burckhardt, *The Civilization of the Renaissance in Italy* (1860), Phaidon Press, 4th edn., 1951, p. 217.
74. E. Gombrich, *In Search of Cultural History* (The Philip Maurice Deneke Lecture 1967), Oxford, 1969, p. 16.
75. *Ibid.*, p. 30.
76. *Ibid.*, pp. 36–7.
77. Giedion, *op. cit.*, p. 18.
78. *Ibid.*, p. 19.
79. *Ibid.*, p. 433.
80. H. Wölfflin, *Renaissance and Baroque* (1888), Fontana Library, 1964, p. 77.
81. Gombrich, *op. cit.*, p. 37.
82. *Ibid.*, p. 46.
83. S. Giedion, *Mechanization Takes Command, a Contribution to Anonymous History,* Oxford University Press, New York, Inc., 1948, p. 394.
84. *Ibid.*, p. 485.
85. *Ibid.*, p. 339.
86. *Ibid.*, pp. 335–6.
87. *Ibid.*, p. 328.
88. *Ibid.*, p. 483.
89. *Ibid.*, p. 8.
90. R.F. Jordan, *Victorian Architecture,* Harmondsworth, 1966, p. 43.
91. *Ibid.*, p. 51.
92. *Ibid.*, p. 50.
93. *Ibid.*, p. 46.
94. *Ibid.*, p. 39.
95. *Ibid.*, p. 61.
96. *Ibid.*, p. 74.
97. *Ibid.*, p. 211.
98. *Ibid.*, p. 224.

99. See D.J. Watkin, *Thomas Hope (1769–1831) and the Neo-Classical Idea*, 1968.
100. Jordan, *op. cit.*, p. 55.
101. *Ibid.*, p. 97.
102. *Ibid.*, p. 147.
103. The Victorian Society *Annual Report*, 1966, p. 3.

Part III. Pevsner

1. N. Pevsner, *Studies in Art, Architecture and Design*, 2 vols., 1968, vol. i, p. 12.
2. *Ibid.*, p. 18.
3. Wölfflin, *op. cit.*, p. 76.
4. Pevsner, *Studies in Art*, p. 20.
5. *Ibid.*, pp. 21–2.
6. *Ibid.*, p. 23.
7. *Ibid.*, p. 28.
8. Wölfflin, *op. cit.*, p. 77.
9. N. Pevsner, 'The Architecture of Mannerism', *The Mint*, 1946, p. 136.
10. *Ibid.*, pp. 116–17.
11. E. Mâle, *L'Art religieux de la fin du moyen âge en France*, Paris (1908), 3rd edn., 1925, p. 495: 'Il y aura encore des artistes chrétiens: il n'y aura plus d'art chrétien.'
12. Republished in Pevsner, *Studies in Art*, vol. i, pp. 35–55.
13. N. Pevsner, *An Outline of European Architecture* (1943), 7th edn., 1963, p. 182.
14. N. Pevsner, *The Leaves of Southwell*, 1945, p. 67.
15. S. Sitwell and N. Pevsner, *German Baroque Sculpture*, 1938, p. 83.
16. Pevsner, *An Outline of European Architecture*, pp. 206–7.
17. Sitwell and Pevsner, *op. cit.*, p. 50.
18. N. Pevsner, *The Englishness of English Art*, 1955, p. 58.
19. *Ibid.*, p. 11.
20. Pevsner, *The Leaves of Southwell*, pp. 63–4.
21. N. Pevsner, 'Architecture in our time', *Listener*, lxxvi, 26 Dec. 1966, p. 953.
22. Pevsner, *Pioneers of the Modern Movement*, p. 41.
23. *Ibid.*, p. 206.
24. E.H. Gombrich, 'Style', *International Encyclopedia of the Social Sciences*, New York, 1968, vol. 15, p. 353.
25. Pevsner, *Pioneers of the Modern Movement*, p. 20.
26. The Victorian Society *Annual*, 1972–3, pp. 8–9.
27. Pevsner, *Pioneers of Modern Design*, p. 23.
28. Pevsner, *Pioneers of the Modern Movement*, p. 24.
29. *Ibid.*, p. 28.

REFERENCES

30. *Ibid.*, p. 30.
31. *Ibid.*, p. 32.
32. *Ibid.*, pp. 33–4.
33. *Ibid.*, p. 34.
34. *Ibid.*, p. 42.
35. See W. Pehnt, 'Gropius the Romantic', *Art Bulletin*, liii, 1971, pp. 379–92, and *Expressionist Architecture*, 1973.
36. Pevsner, *Pioneers of the Modern Movement*, p. 84. My italics.
37. *Ibid.*, p. 91.
38. *Ibid.*, p. 193.
39. See W. Laqueur, *Young Germany, a History of the German Youth Movement*, 1962.
40. Pevsner, *Pioneers of the Modern Movement*, p. 143.
41. *Ibid.*, p. 145. My italics.
42. Lethaby, *Form in Civilisation*, p. 17.
43. Pevsner, *Pioneers of the Modern Movement*, p. 149. My italics.
44. *Ibid.*, p. 163–4.
45. *Ibid.*, p. 53.
46. *Ibid.*, p. 54.
47. *Ibid.*, p. 55.
48. *Ibid.*, p. 56.
49. *Ibid.*, p. 60.
50. *Ibid.*, p. 66.
51. *Ibid.*, p. 71. My italics.
52. Pevsner, *Pioneers of Modern Design*, p. 89. My italics.
53. Pevsner, *Pioneers of the Modern Movement*, pp. 110–11.
54. *Ibid.*, p. 117.
55. Pevsner, *Pioneers of Modern Design*, p. 112.
56. Pevsner, *Pioneers of the Modern Movement*, pp. 165–6.
57. *Ibid.*, p. 173.
58. *Ibid.*, p. 181.
59. G. Scott, *The Architecture of Humanism* (1914), 2nd edn., 1924, p. 176.
60. Pevsner, *Pioneers of the Modern Movement*, p. 176.
61. *Ibid.*, p. 202.
62. *Ibid.*, p. 180.
63. *Ibid.*, pp. 179–80.
64. *Ibid.*, p. 204.
65. *Ibid.*, pp. 204–7.
66. Pevsner, *Pioneers of Modern Design*, p. 217.
67. Pevsner, *Pioneers of the Modern Movement*, p. 193.
68. Pevsner, *Pioneers of Modern Design*, p. 202.
69. *Ibid.*, p. 18.

70. *Ibid.*, p. 214.
71. Pevsner, *Pioneers of the Modern Movement*, p. 124.
72. *Ibid.*, p. 127.
73. Pevsner, *An Enquiry*, p. 112.
74. *Ibid.*, p. 113.
75. *Ibid.*, p. 138.
76. *Ibid.*, p. 171.
77. *Ibid.*, p. 168.
78. *Ibid.*, p. 11.
79. *Ibid.*, pp. 123–5.
80. *Ibid.*, p. 215.
81. *Ibid.*, p. 201.
82. *Ibid.*, p. 212.
83. N. Pevsner, 'A Pioneer Designer: Arthur H. Mackmurdo', *Architectural Review*, lxxxiii, Mar. 1938, pp. 141–3; 'George Walton, his Life and Work', *R.I.B.A. Journal*, xlvi, 3 Apr. 1939, pp. 537–48; 'Patient Progress: the life work of Frank Pick', *Architectural Review*, xcii, Aug. 1942, pp. 31–48.
84. Pevsner, *Studies in Art*, p. 183.
85. *Ibid.*, p. 191.
86. *Ibid.*, p. 202.
87. *Ibid.*, p. 197.
88. *Ibid.*, p. 209.
89. Pugin, *An Apology*, p. 39.
90. Pevsner, *An Outline of European Architecture*, pp. 218–20.
91. *Ibid.*, pp. 201–2.
92. P. Thompson, *William Butterfield*, 1971, p. 6.
93. N. Pevsner, *The Buildings of England, London, vol. i, The Cities of London and Westminster* (1957), 3rd edn., 1973, p. 111.
94. *Ibid.*, pp. 225, 245, 255, 580, and 593–4.
95. Pevsner, *Studies in Art*, vol. ii, p. 243.
96. *Ibid.*, p. 244.
97. *Ibid.*, p. 255.
98. *Historismus und bildende Kunst, Vorträge und Diskussion im Oktober 1963 in München und Schloss Anif*, Munich, 1965, p. 74.
99. *Ibid.*, p. 109.
100. K. Popper, *The Poverty of Historicism* (first published as articles 1944–5), 1957, pp. 160 and 10.
101. K. Popper, *Conjectures and Refutations*, p. 342.
102. See *The Philosophy of Karl Popper*, ed. P.A. Schilpp, 2 vols., Illinois, 1974, vol. ii, p. 1174.
103. *Ibid.*, p. 925.

References

Conclusion

1. H. Honour, *Neo-Classicism*, 1968, p. 15.
2. H.-R. Hitchcock, *Architecture, Nineteenth and Twentieth Centuries* (1958), 3rd edn., 1968, p. 408.
3. Pevsner, *An Outline of European Architecture*, p. 209.
4. '. . . ein unbegreiflicher Scherz des grossen Meisters', on p. 165 of Burckhardt's *Die Renaissance in Italien* which appeared as Part I of vol. iv (Stuttgart, 1867) of F.T. Kugler's *Geschichte der Baukunst*, 4 vols., Stuttgart, 1856–72.

EPILOGUE

The Critical Reaction

Published in the autumn of 1977, *Morality and Architecture* was at first largely ignored by the architectural establishment whose assumptions it questioned. However, a flood of publicity followed an enthusiastic editorial, called 'The Time Bomb', which Denys Sutton devoted to it in the October issue of *Apollo*. Sutton claimed that it

> deserves to become a set book in art schools and University art history departments. But will it? Dr Watkin's exposure of the fallacies of the collectivists and the 'modernists' will prove too much for many officials and teachers, and certainly for the politicians. In some countries Dr Watkin would be well advised to hire a bodyguard or even to slip across the frontier! He deserves to be congratulated for standing up for intellectual freedom.

From those professionals the book also had, initially, an encouraging reception. Thus Lance Wright, editor of the leading architectural journal, *The Architectural Review*, reviewed it in November, claiming that it is 'obsessive and mischievous but affords an excellent introduction to the times we are now in'. One of its keenest supporters was Sir John Betjeman, who had long nourished a near-obsessive dislike of Pevsner for his approach to English architecture and his promotion of modernist design in historic settings.[1] Reviewing *Morality and Architecture* for *Books and Bookmen*, Betjeman hailed it as 'A modern version of Geoffrey Scott's *The*

---

[1] See Timothy Mowl, *Stylistic Cold Wars: Betjeman versus Pevsner*, London 2000.

Architecture of Humanism', claiming in Suttonesque language that it 'is like a bomb', and finally choosing it as his favourite reading of 1977 in *The Sunday Times* in December. Even more valuable support came from Sir John Summerson, who wrote to me in December 1977:

> Re-reading it has been a very great pleasure. I admire the book greatly. It is the most important piece of writing on the philosophy of architecture that has appeared for a very long time. But do I agree with everything you say? Well, yes, I think I do. I have the feeling that you have written an obituary of ideas which have wilted and died *without many of us realising that this is what has happened!* . . . I can't imagine that you will be seriously challenged . . . Not even – but I wonder, I wonder – by N. Pevsner! . . . I do think your critique of Pevsner is absolutely brilliant. And you have written with such elegance that it is in a way a tribute to the great man. What I don't much care for is your piece on R. Furneaux Jordan. It strikes a discordant note. He is foot-note size, as you well know . . . What I *did* like and what *ought* perhaps to have had a separate heading was the piece on *Space, Time and Architecture*, a book I have always detested. Your disposal of it is admirable.[2]

After Summerson's death in 1992, I came across his copy of *Morality and Architecture* in the library of the Prince of Wales's Institute of Architecture. I was interested to see that his annotations on it, apparently made at the time of writing his letter to me, contained the phrase, 'it has never occurred to me to think of any architectural theory as morally right or wrong.'

At the same time I received support from some modern architects, including Sir Denys Lasdun, who wrote in the course of his letter: 'I much enjoyed *Morality and Architecture* and subscribe to its central theme.'[3] The leading engineer, Sir Ove Arup, wrote:

---

[2] Sir John Summerson to the author, 28 December 1977.
[3] Sir Denys Lasdun to the author, 15 December 1977.

I have read it with great pleasure. I entirely agree with your main thesis. That most of what is paraded as 'Architectural Theory' is a load of nonsense to put it crudely, is an opinion I have held for more than thirty years . . . Now, when this opinion is expressed by a professional art historian who can quote chapter and verse and prove his case, and not just by an engineer, I hope some notice will be taken of it.[4]

Quinlan Terry wrote to me:

Students and Rome Scholars who have not been totally immersed in Pevsner are avid supporters. I gather it is the R.I.B.A. bookshop best seller. But I am also interested to note how some of our mutual friends in the art-historical world (mentioning no names!) are critical and call it 'hitting below the belt'. It is becoming a touchstone by which I sort the architectural sheep from the architectural goats.[5]

Valued support came from other varied sources, including an article by Paul Johnson in the *Daily Telegraph* on 17 December 1977, and a letter from Joe Mordaunt Crook in the same month, saying

I read *Morality and Architecture* with immense pleasure: a polemic in the real Peterhouse tradition. Nobody has yet asked me to review it, and I am in the dark as to who has been commissioned by the *T.L.S.* You are, of course, up against the Lib-Lab gerontocracy.[6]

In a review by Sir Osbert Lancaster, definitely not a member of that particular gerontocracy, in *The Cambridge Review* of 3 February 1978, he claimed that 'Dr Watkin has earned the gratitude of all who care for firmness, commodity and, particularly, delight'.

Following the encouragement I had received from Summerson and Gombrich, I was anxious to hear from the third in the great trio of scholars whose opinions I most valued, Sir Karl Popper. He wrote to me of the book:

---

[4] Sir Ove Arup to the author, 31 January 1978.
[5] Quinlan Terry to the author, 8 February 1978.
[6] Dr J. Mordaunt Crook to the author, 7 December 1977.

I find this important. The irrelevance and emptiness of the Zeitgeist philosophy is shown very powerfully in your book. Historicism, the wish to be a leader of fashion and ahead of one's time, has, I fear, killed music and painting. I admire much of the work of Gropius and Frank Lloyd Wright, in spite of their horrible historicist utterances (of which I did not know) . . . Like Hegelianism and Marxism, modernism in art was (and possibly still is) a religious movement . . . I think that the truth is that great architects, like great musicians, or great novelists, are very rare. And thus most want a 'new style' for copying.[7]

What strikes me, looking back on the succession of events of over twenty years ago, is that though major figures such as Arup, Gombrich, Lasdun, Popper, and Summerson, agreed with me in private, they felt unable, for whatever reason, to say anything supportive in public. This would have been helpful in view of attacks such as that by the philosopher Richard Wollheim who argued in the *Architectural Review* symposium that because I was 'a writer who is without any sense of the decline in architecture which was experienced around the turn of the century', I could not see why modernism was a necessary reaction to it. He might have taken a different view of the quality of architecture at that time had he read John Summerson's pamphlet, *The Turn of the Century: Architecture in Britain Around 1900* (Glasgow University Press 1976).

So much for the sheep, in Quinlan Terry's phrase; now for the goats. They were beginning to form quite a herd. The book was unusually made the subject of a Symposium in the *Architectural Review* in February 1978 in which four people were invited to give their opinions: the philosophers Roger Scruton and Richard Wollheim, Kenneth Campbell, the former housing architect to the London County Council, and the architectural writer Charles Jencks. The only fully supportive contribution came from Scruton, who argued that it is 'the moral significance of architecture that makes the moralism of the Modern Movement so distasteful.' Campbell, an unreconstructed modernist, argued that 'most people

---

[7] Sir Karl Popper to the author, 28 February 1978.

with hearts' believe in building a new society 'based on equality', an equality which will, apparently, be furthered by 'honest, simple, functional building'.

The biggest goat in the herd lined up against *Morality and Architecture* was Reyner Banham (1922–88) in the *Times Literary Supplement* of 17 February 1978. An historian and critic who had been, like me, a pupil of Pevsner, he was a tireless advocate of the avant-garde, of New Brutalism and the Machine Aesthetic. His review was prompted by his outrage at any attack on modernist values and particularly on Pevsner on the grounds that he had 'got it right', i.e. 'backed the winners'. Banham savaged the book as a product of 'that kind of vindictiveness of which only Christians seem capable'.[8] So much for Summerson writing to me that 'I can't imagine that you will be seriously challenged'![9] Nonetheless, the original edition of *Morality and Architecture* was reprinted in 1978, translated into Italian, French, Spanish, and Japanese, and reissued as a paperback by Chicago University Press. I was invited to undertake a lecture tour in America in the early part of 1980 to explain my ideas which I duly did at the universities of Princeton, Yale, Harvard, and Columbia, and the Rhode Island School of Design. The message seemed less controversial and more acceptable in the USA than in England, for modernism had never been promoted there with the ruthless exclusivity which had prevailed in Britain and the Continent.

The Position Today

During the 1980s support for traditional architectre came from the Prince of Wales, who had come to feel that the soulless products of modernist urbanism were damaging the lives of the British people,

---

[8] In a review reprinted as late as 1996 in *A Critic Writes: Essays by Reyner Banham* (Berkeley and Los Angeles, pp. 216–22).

[9] Letters to the *Times Literary Supplement* from Peregrine Horden, Hugh Plommer, and Anthony West subsequently defended me from Banham's criticism.

his future subjects. His speech to the Royal Institute of British Architects in 1984, describing the design for the addition to the National Gallery by Ahrends, Burton and Koralek as a 'monstrous carbuncle', struck a tremendous chord with the public though outraged the architectural establishment. At a meeting in July 1987 the Prince discussed his ideas with a small group of architects and historians, and suggested to John Simpson that he should design a new setting for St Paul's Cathedral on the site of William Holford's grim Paternoster Square for which some appallingly insensitive replacements had just been proposed. The favourable reception which Simpson's eventual classical scheme for Paternoster Square received when it was exhibited to the public was one of the many factors which encouraged the Prince to make a BBC film, *A Vision of Britain*, in October 1988. After this film, he received nearly 5,000 letters, of which an overwhelming majority agreed with him. The BBC invited viewers to send in pictures of buildings which they felt had ruined the towns they lived in. When hundreds responded, the BBC decided to put them on public exhibition, the Building Centre having refused to exhibit them, and *Building News* eventually dismissing the exhibition as a 'smelly little show'.[10]

Morality and Architecture was well received in its Italian translation and I was invited to give papers at two revisionist conferences in Italy in 1991–2. At the first conference, on classical architecture in Europe and America from 1920 to 1940, I spoke on style and politics in British architecture in the 1930s.[11] The conference was organized by the Centro Internazionale di Studi di Architettura Andrea Palladio at Vicenza under the direction of Giorgio Ciucci, a Professor of Architecture at Rome University. Ciucci, who had invited George Hersey, Gavin Stamp, and me, is one of a growing group of Italian scholars who seek to end what they see as the conspiracy of silence about the countless classically inspired buildings put up in Italy throughout the 1930s. Such buildings have been

---

[10] The Prince of Wales, *A Vision of Britain*, London 1989, p. 8.
[11] Published in Giorgio Ciucci, ed., *Classicismo – Classicismi: Architettura Europa/America 1920–1940*, Milan 1995, pp. 185–95.

ignored by historians because they are 'politically incorrect' through supposed identification with Mussolini. Bruno Zevi (1918–2000), architectural historian and editor of the leading journal, *L'Architettura, Cronache e Storia*, devoted a succession of editorials in 1991–92 to hysterical and violent abuse of the organizers of this conference whose only fault was that it was devoted to dispassionate investigation of the architecture of undesirable political regimes. He dismissed the classical architecture of the 1930s as 'a crackpot subject . . . stupid and obscene', describing the organiszers of the conference as 'wallowing in a cultural sewer' composed of 'shit, muck, vomit, and spittle' which they 'will have to scrape up from the ground with their hands and smear on their faces, on their bodies, and on their conscience.'[12]

Despite this extraordinary onslaught, I gave a paper at a second conference, on 'Nikolaus Pevsner: historian of art, architecture, and design', in the Faculty of Architecture at the Polytechnic of Milan in 1992, organized by Fulvio Irace who has since published a study of the largely classical twentieth-century architect, Giovanni Muzio.[13] The conference was specially notable for the contribution by Marlite Halbertsma on Pevsner's debt to Pinder which we have already noted above. She showed the influence on Pevsner of the determinist approach of Pinder who saw, for example, 'all late mediaeval sculpture as a single, albeit very complicated, movement towards Dürer', and was confident that 'the "character" of nations can be distinguished in European art.' She argued that Pinder and Pevsner 'believe that the practice of art history is a vocation that should lead to a new national or social consciousness. Pinder saw this in Germany and things German, Pevsner in modern society'.[14]

---

[12] *L'Architettura, Cronache e Storia*, June 1991, pp. 504–5, and February 1992, p. 85. The Italian words used by Zevi include 'cacca' and 'merda', crude slang meaning 'crap' and 'shit'.

[13] Fulvio Irace, *Giovanni Muzio 1893–1982, Opere*, Milan 1994.

[14] Marlite Halbertsma, in a shortened version of her paper published as 'Nikolaus Pevsner and the End of a Tradition: The Legacy of Wilhelm Pinder', *Apollo*, February 1993, pp. 107–9. My own paper on Pevsner and Historicism had appeared in *Apollo* in September 1992.

The belief in the need to express the *Zeitgeist* persists despite the changing character of society, so that we find today the architect Rem Koolhaas, winner of the Pritzker Prize and considered one of the foremost current practitioners, arguing that modern architecture has to express the chaos of the era of the millennium.[15] Winckelmann and Frank Lloyd Wright both argued that the, very different, architecture they admired was the expression of democracy, while Allan Greenberg, one of the finest of modern classical architects, has also argued fallaciously, that, 'there is a fundamental, consanguine relationship between the ideals of classical architecture and democracy'.[16] However, the language of the orders in ancient Greece was supported materially by slavery and symbolically by magic and animal sacrifice.

Also, Greenberg's assumption about the identification of architectural style with politics led, ironically, to the abandonment of classical architecture after the Second World War, especially in Germany, on the assumption that it was irrevocably associated with Nazism. Indeed, it is still extremely difficult to practise in the classical manner in Germany or even in Italy, as we have seen from the hysterical outburst of Bruno Zevi against studying classical architecture, let alone practising it.

Astonishingly, the architectural writer Jules Lubbock could claim of classical architecture as late as 1987, that 'its associations with Nazism make it eternally unacceptable'.[17] A wiser approach has been adopted in a recent study of the rich classical architecture of the Stalinist era whose authors claim that, 'Despite all the understandable prejudices against the bloody history of the Stalin cult, we cannot deny the powerful creative quality of some of its art.'[18] Indeed, if the classical language is timeless, it is wrong to claim that

---

[15] Rem Koolhaas, *S, M, L, XL [Small, Medium, Large, Extra-Large]* (1995), Koln 1997.

[16] Allan Greenberg, *Selected Works*, London 1995, p. 13.

[17] Jules Lubbock, 'Politics of the Portico', *New Statesman*, 1 May 1987, pp. 20–22.

[18] Alexei Tarkhanov and Sergei Kavtaradze, *Stalinist Architecture*, London 1992, p. 6.

it is an expression of whatever social and political system we happen to favour. It is sometimes thought that classicism was somehow uniquely hijacked by the dictators of the 1930s, but it should be remembered that the same stripped classical style was adopted in America at the same time.[19]

In her study of Mies van Der Rohe, Elaine Hochman asked the key questions of whether,

> when viewed through the telescope of time, issues of morality fade as the art endures. While of undoubted concern to his contemporaries, the question of whether or not Justinian, the creator of the magnificent Hagia Sofia, was a 'good' ruler now seems quite irrelevant. To the slave labor that built them, the Greek temples we now so admire surely did not seem so beautiful – nor do the Romanesque cathedrals seem today marred by having been built with the booty of the Crusades.[20]

The planner and theorist, Léon Krier (b. 1946), whose numerous urban schemes have included Poundbury, Dorset, for the Prince of Wales, has been a passionate opposer of the damaging and limiting impact of the *Zeitgeist* in architecture. He asked whether 'in a revolutionary and bloody age', like the twentieth century, 'should architecture be as a consequence aggressive and deadly?'[21] Krier has also shown how the modernist notion of 'honesty' in architecture, including the notion that it should be true to the spirit of its age, has now had a damaging effect on the restoration of historic buildings. He cites as evidence the Charter of Venice formulated during the Second International Congress of Architects and Technicians of Historic Buildings in Venice in 1964 which was adopted by the International Council for Monuments and Sites (ICOMOS) in 1965. This insists that 'Replacement of missing parts . . . must be distinguishable from the original so that restoration does not falsify

---

[19] See, for example, *Public Buildings: Architecture under the Public Works Administration 1933–39* (1939) reprinted 1986.

[20] Hochman, *op. cit.*, p. 314.

[21] Léon Krier, *Architecture: Choice or Fate*, London 1998, p. 71.

the artistic or historic evidence', and that 'All reconstruction work should . . . be ruled out *a priori* . . . The materials used for integration should be recognisable.' This leads to the preservation of 'honest' fragments rather than, as Krier puts it, 'of masterpieces in their organic and organisational coherence'.[22]

Krier has not been entirely alone in condemning this destructive influence of modernist theory. Modernist architecture has also been questioned by Jane Jacobs in *The Death and Life of Great American Cities* (New York 1961), by Robert Venturi in *Complexity and Contradiction in Architecture* (New York 1966), and in *Learning from Las Vegas: The Forgotten Symbolism of Architectural Form* (Cambridge, Mass., 1972), and, most decisively, by Peter Blake in *Form Follows Fiasco: Why Modern Architecture Hasn't Worked* (Boston, Mass., 1977), a remarkable volte-face by an apostate disciple of Chermayeff. Echoing the 'fallacies' exposed by Geoffrey Scott in *The Architecture of Humanism* (1914), Blake condemned the ten 'fantasies' of modernism which he identified as 'Function, The Open Plan, Purity, Technology, The Skyscraper, The Ideal City, Mobility, Zoning, Housing, and Form.' Though ignored by the architectural establishment, this book should be compulsory reading for all creators of malfunctioning modernist buildings such as Norman Foster and Richard Rogers.

Few of these books had, however, considered the question of the weakness of the historical and philosophical foundations of modernist theory which I attempted to address. Exceptions were Roger Scruton's *The Aesthetics of Architecture* (1979) and the massive study by William Westfall and Robert Van Pelt, *Architectural Principles in the Age of Historicism* (1991), which investigated the relationship between architectural history and the current practice of architecture. This originated in what Westfall saw as the architectural damage wrought in Chicago from the 1970s by modernist doctrines. The belief in the timeless nature of the classical language of architecture which led Westfall and Van Pelt to 'reject the modernist assumption that architecture has a relationship only with a

---

[22] *Ibid.*, pp. 73–5.

specific place and time', enabled them to explain 'the destructive role orthodox architectural history plays in our cities'.[23]

Yet this small but strong tradition of critical questioning of modernism has had little influence. Shortly after the publication of Roger Scruton's *Aesthetics of Architecture* (1979), the Bartlett School of Architecture devoted a day-long seminar to criticism of it and of *Morality and Architecture* to which neither of us was invited.

Scruton considers that,

> We had been perceived as identifying the pernicious influence of an aesthetic and political establishment which continues to hold power today. Leading architects posturing as egalitarians with an ideal of human society, are allowed to muscle all competition out of their environment while making vast financial gains. Who wants these buildings except those who are making money out of them?

Roger Scruton encourages me to distinguish more clearly than in *Morality and Architecture* between morality and moralism. He points out that those I criticize were moralists who wanted architecture to moralize on their behalf though they did not want to pay the cost of their so-called morality. Not for them life in a high-rise block on a London housing estate: that was for the proles. Scruton argues that,

> Since architecture forms the background to our principal forms of social life, it can further that life or impede it. The buildings that the modernists justified are actually immoral in depriving our cities of a human appearance, a peaceful ambience, and the marks of a negotiated human life. They are responsible for driving the people from our cities. Thus, architecture has a moral function but only by virtue of its own *intrinsic* nature as an art of design, obedient to aesthetic values and to the law of aesthetic compromise. When we try to make an architecture into a direct form of moralising, a sermon in

---

[23] R. Van Pelt and C.W. Westfall, *Architectural Principles in the Age of Historicism*, New Haven and London, 1991, p. [vi].

concrete, we destroy its nature as architecture. And the result is a
moral and therefore a social disaster.[24]

The year 2000 saw the publication of a brilliant book by Timothy
Mowl, *Stylistic Cold Wars: Betjeman versus Pevsner*, in which he wrote
that, 'I would not have written this book without the stimulus of a
brave book [*Morality and Architecture*] published at a cowardly time.
It posed questions about Pevsner and his influence that have not
been answered, that have been shuffled away by those who find
them inconvenient.' He showed how Betjeman and Pevsner exercised more influence on architecture and its appreciation than
anyone since Ruskin, yet the learned Pevsner held Betjeman in low
esteem while the jolly Betjeman developed an antipathy towards
Pevsner, the solemn German emigré, that at times was obsessional.
The many ironies in the lives and achievements of these two men
include the fact that Betjeman was responsible for ending the
climate prevailing in the 1950s and 60s, which condemned any later
nineteenth century building as 'a Victorian monstrosity'. Pevsner,
by contrast, even though he became Chairman of the Victorian
Society, had little sympathy for the more violent forms of Victorian
architecture, so anxious was he to move into what was, for him, the
rationalist perfection of the International Modern architecture of
the 1930s. Mowl's book received varied reactions, like *Morality and
Architecture*, including powerful backing from Simon Jenkins and
James Stevens Curl.

Anything that contributes to debate must be welcomed, especially when the orthodoxy that architecture 'must express the spirit
of its age' dominates the architectural establishment represented by
the RIBA, Richard Rogers, Norman Foster, and even English
Heritage. One example of the language used in these quarters will
give the flavour of the whole. An essay on new galleries in London
claimed how, in the premises of the Gilbert Collection which had
just been opened in the remodelled ground floor and vaults of one
of the greatest neo-classical buildings in England, Somerset House

---

[24] Professor Roger Scruton to the author, 12 July 2000.

(1776–96), by Sir William Chambers, 'The architects Inskip and Jenkins have been anxious to avoid historicising fakery, and have gone for "honest" exposed brickwork with a metal staircase and mezzanine'. Of the new galleries at the National Portrait Gallery by Jones and Dixon it was stated that: 'The architecture is of the clean, neo-modernist variety, and it is refreshing to find an addition to a historic museum building in Britain which makes so few nods . . . to "heritage"'.[25]

It is important to question the instinctive condemnation of all traditional work as 'historicising fakery', for why would it be fakery to adopt the classical language in the year 2000, but not in the 1850s when Sir James Pennethorne added the vast west wing to Somerset House in a manner owing much to his close study of Chambers? At the same time, Pennethorne incorporated iron girders and columns and a glass roof,[26] demonstrating that the incorporation of modern technology need not be expressed externally. Pennethorne was congratulated in a testimonial of 1 July 1856, signed by over seventy architects including Sir Charles Barry, C.R. Cockerell, Owen Jones, Salvin, and Digby Wyatt, who wrote, 'you have done full justice to the genius of Chambers . . . [and] adapted these additions to a difficult site'.[27]

How different was the position a century later when a giant block of abrasive reeded concrete was added in 1966–71 from designs by Troup, Steele, and Mathews, on the east side of Somerset House, as an extension of King's College which had been built in the 1830s by Robert Smirke in the style of Chambers. Was it also 'historicising fakery' for Girolamo and Carlo Rainaldi to build the Palazzo Nuovo on the Capitol in Rome in 1644–54, based on designs made over a century before by Michelangelo; for Henry Yevele to build the nave of Westminster Abbey in the late four-

---

[25] *Burlington Magazine*, June 2000, p. 343. However, it is rare to find a modern addition to a museum which pays attention to the style of the existing building.
[26] See Geoffrey Tyack, *Sir James Pennethorne and the Making of Victorian London*, Cambridge 1992, p. 92.
[27] *The Builder*, 2 August 1856, p. 425.

teenth century, following the French Gothic style established at the east end over a century before by Henry of Reyns; for Christopher Wren and Nicholas Hawksmoor to continue in the Gothic style Christ Church, Oxford, and Westminster Abbey respectively; or in their harmonious additions to the Royal Hospital at Greenwich, for Wren to follow the style of John Webb and, more remarkably, for Daniel Alexander in 1807 to follow that of Inigo Jones?[28]

The hostility towards inspiration from the past makes it impossible to understand the Renaissance with its tradition of imitating and copying antique works. In a discussion about the Renaissance on Radio 4 in June 2000, Frances Ames-Lewis criticized the view that this tradition should be dismissed as pastiche. Melvyn Bragg agreed, suggesting that otherwise someone might say, 'I've got a fake. It's by Michelangelo.'

Yet no amount of historical evidence or philosophical argument has so far entirely shifted the depressing effluvia of yesterday's modernist belief that if you add on to an historic building you must be 'truthful' by not harmonizing with its existing style. Indeed, the cause of classical and traditional architecture has been temporarily eclipsed in Britain by the unexpected millennial fillip given to Rogers, Foster, and their High Tech orthodoxy. Moreover, as has already been mentioned, no school of architecture in Britain teaches the practice of traditional and classical architecture, despite the fact that, as was demonstrated in a survey conducted in 1998 by the architect Robert Adam (b. 1948), houses in traditional styles are preferred by the overwhelming majority of the British public.[29]

Nonetheless, the architectural press normally ignores traditional designs by architects in Britain such as Robert Adam, Liam O'Connor, Demetri Porphyrios, John Simpson, and Quinlan Terry, in Italy by Pier-Carlo Bontempi and Gabriele Tagliaventi, and, most notably, in the USA by John Blatteau, Allan Greenberg,

---

[28] Pevsner found it 'astonishing' that Yevele 'did not insist on something in his own style or the style of his day' (*The Buildings of England, London, vol. i, The Cities of London and Westminster* (1957) rev. ed., Harmondsworth 1973, p. 405).

[29] The Popular Housing Forum, *Report Number One* (Winchester, Autumn, 1998).

Jorge Hernandez, Richard Sammons, Thomas Gordon Smith, and Robert Stern; nor is attention paid to the burgeoning movement for traditional urbanism in America, including the new towns by Andres Duany and Elizabeth Plater-Zyberk with their associated building codes. The work of this new movement involves architects of all ages from all European countries, as well as from the USA, where traditional and classical architecture is taught in the Schools of Architecture at Notre Dame University and the University of Miami. It has been extensively published in books edited by Gabriele Tagliaventi, including *Architecture and Urbanism for the European City* (Bologna 1992), *A Vision of Europe: Urban Renaissance* (Bologna 1996), and *The Other Modern 1900–2000: Classical and Traditional Architecture in the Construction of Cities from 1900–2000* (Bologna 2000). Robert Stern, the prolific classical architect who is Professor at the Yale School of Architecture, supported me by claiming that, 'the anti-Classicism of this century was as much the result of an hermetic aestheticism as the Classicism it so derided . . . What was largely a matter of taste was pursued as an issue of moral essence.'[30] He even suggested that it was less the artefacts than the concepts of modernism which must be questioned.

This corpus of building and theory is encouraging, for nothing like it existed in 1977 when *Morality and Architecture* first appeared. However, it still represents a small minority of what is built and is ignored in the professional architectural press. In general, traditional forms and ornament are banned from new buildings: if used, they are ridiculed as immoral pastiche in a lack of humility which threatens to cut us off from our past. Fortunately, many do not share this worship of the new, the most admired cities being those like Paris, Rome, Venice, and Prague, whose centres are not yet wrecked by modernist buildings reflecting 'the spirit of their age'.[31]

---

[30] Robert A.M. Stern, *Modern Classicism*, London 1988, p. 282.
[31] Though Paris is by no means unscathed: see Louis Chevalier, *The Assassination of Paris*, Chicago and London 1994.

Index

INDEX

INDEX

Index

INDEX